P9-DGS-374

Twayne's United States Authors Series

Sylvia E. Bowman, *Editor*

INDIANA UNIVERSITY

Jesse Stuart

JESSE STUART

By RUEL E. FOSTER

West Virginia University

 140

CARNEGIE LIBRARY
LIVINGSTONE COLLEGE
SALISBURY, N. C. 28144

Twayne Publishers, Inc.   ::   New York

Copyright © 1968 by Twayne Publishers, Inc.

All Rights Reserved

Library of Congress Catalog Card Number: 68-24298

MANUFACTURED IN THE UNITED STATES OF AMERICA

818.52
F756

73310

For my wife
MARGARET
and my aunt
MISS EFFIE FOSTER

Preface

THIS STUDY is a book-length literary assessment of Jesse Stuart. A writer of undoubted merit, Stuart has been largely ignored by serious contemporary critics, probably because his work lies outside the currently fashionable modes of irony, ambivalence, and nihilism. The present book is an attempt to bring Stuart into the ken of serious readers and critics, and to offer a balanced presentation of his total work as an autobiographical writer, poet, and fictionist.

Ordinarily an evaluative book on a writer would devote at least one chapter to his life. Stuart has obviated the need for such a chapter by his own autobiographical works. As a result, Chapter 1, "The Autobiographical Writings: Mountain Gloom and Mountain Glory," performs the biographical function. The four autobiographical books discussed cover the major events and concerns of Stuart's life from childhood to adulthood and on to his climactic heart attack at the age of forty-nine.

In Chapter 2, "The Poetry: A Glory from the Earth," Stuart's earliest and most sustained literary enthusiasm—poetry—is discussed; and analyses and evaluations are made of the five volumes of poetry he has so far published. Chapter 3, "The Short Stories: Tales of Shan and Others," brings together the salient characteristics of Stuart as a writer as demonstrated in his most popular form, the short story. He is very prolific in this medium, and his best stories have about them a great freshness and originality.

Chapter 4, "The Major Novels: Children of the Earth," considers some of those longer fictional works in which Stuart takes up the fullest delineations of his W-Hollow world and the "dirt-colored men" who inhabit it. An attempt is made here, as in the precedent chapters, to give a brief summation of the content of the works as well as an evaluation of their literary merit. Other longer fictional works by Stuart are treated in Chapter 5, "The Minor Novels."

Finally, Chapter 6, "Elegist of a Lost World," brings together certain generalizations about Stuart's total impact as a writer and projects the future of his reputation. It is an attempt to avoid both the blindness of those academic critics who have completely ignored him and the uncritical adulation of some journalistic reviewers. Stuart has created a fictional place—W-

Hollow—and wedged it firmly and lastingly in the literary topography of our country. It is there cheek by jowl with Faulkner's Yoknapatawpha County. This achievement alone would make Stuart's work important and worthy of critical evaluation.

RUEL E. FOSTER

West Virginia University

Acknowledgments

My chief debt in the preparation of the present volume is to Mr. Jesse Stuart, who answered many, many questions and provided copies of letters, articles, and manuscripts, giving information which I could not otherwise have obtained. I thank him warmly for this generous help.

This book was put together during the past four years under conditions of considerable academic stress and strain. I am very grateful to my academic superiors for giving me some reduction in teaching load during intervals of this writing period, thus making it possible for me to complete the book. I would mention especially my former chairman, Dr. J. P. Brawner, Dean Carl Frasure of the College of Arts and Sciences, and Dr. John Golay, former Provost of the University. I greatly appreciate their help. Professor Donovan Bond, Director of Development, was instrumental in securing a summer grant from the Benedum Foundation which permitted me to advance the progress of the book markedly. I proffer my warmest thanks.

Dr. Robert Munn, Director of the University Libraries, and his staff obtained theses, microfilm, books, and xeroxed materials with unfailing courtesy and dispatch. It is a rare pleasure to work in a library operated by Dr. Munn and his associates. I constantly availed myself of the expert technical knowledge of Dr. John Caruso, who is a national authority on the history of the Appalachian area, in my treatment of Stuart, who is one of the greatest writers indigenous to Appalachia. I recall with pleasure and gratitude our many fine talks on this subject.

From the earliest rough sketches to the finished manuscript, Mrs. Jane Lemley, our departmental secretary, has handled the typing with unfailing efficiency, kindness, and good humor. For her help and her forbearance I express here my warmest thanks.

Vanderbilt University Press has kindly granted me permission to reprint "Jesse Stuart, Short Story Writer" from its *Reality and Myth* (1964). This article appears in the present volume, with only the first paragraph changed, as "The Short Stories: Tales of Shan and Others." I am grateful for this permission.

Professor Hensley C. Woodbridge proved an unfailing help

to me through his excellent bibliography of works by and about Stuart. Dr. Sylvia E. Bowman, TUSAS editor, was unusually discerning in her suggestions of needed revisions, and very generous in allocating to the present work time from her busy schedule. I am much indebted to both.

Finally, my profoundest thanks to my wife Margaret and to my aunt, Miss Effie Foster, for their enduring love and concern.

Contents

Chronology

1907   August 8, Jesse Hilton Stuart born in Greenup County, Kentucky; the first of seven children born to Mitchell and Martha Hilton Stuart.

1926   Graduated from Greenup High School. Entered Lincoln Memorial University at Harrogate, Tennessee.

1929   Graduated with a B.A. degree from Lincoln Memorial.

1929-
1930   Principal of Warnock High School. August, 1930, received copies of his first published book, *Harvest of Youth*.

1930-
1931   Principal of Greenup High.

1931-
1932   Spent school year at Vanderbilt University. September, 1931, entered graduate school to take master's degree in English.

1932   Wrote first draft of *Beyond Dark Hills* as a term paper for Dr. Edwin Mims. May, left Vanderbilt without taking his degree. September 16, took position as superintendent of Greenup County Schools.

1933   May, accepted principalship of McKell High School; held it for the next four years.

1934   October 14, *Man with a bull-tongue Plow*, December, his second book published. Wrote in forty-eight hours three major short stories; all published in major magazines. This confirmed his short story vocation.

1936   April 17, *Head O' W-Hollow* published.

1937   July, sailed for Scotland on a Guggenheim Fellowship.

1938   April 18, *Beyond Dark Hills*. July, returned to New York City. September, started teaching in a high school in Portsmouth, Ohio. October 1, attacked and beaten over the head by an enemy.

1939   October 14, married to Naomi Deane Norris.

1940   April 22, published *Trees of Heaven*, his first novel.

1941   January, received the $500 award of American Institute of Arts and Letters for his contribution to literature in 1940. March, *Men of the Mountains*.

1942   August 20, his only child, Jessica Jane, born.

1943 November 24, *Taps For Private Tussie*. Received the $2,500 Thomas Jefferson Southern Award for the best Southern book of the year.

1944 July 12, commissioned Lieutenant (j.g.) in U.S. Naval Reserve. February 21, *Mongrel Mettle*. September 26, *Album of Destiny*.

1945 December 31, discharged from the Navy.

1946 March 8, *Foretaste of Glory*. October 14, *Tales From the Plum Grove Hills*.

1949 September 26, *The Thread That Runs So True*.

1950 National Education Association voted *The Thread That Runs So True* "the most important book of 1949." May 1, *Hie to the Hunters*. October 24, *Clearing in the Sky and Other Stories*.

1951 May 11, his mother died; buried in Plum Grove Churchyard.

1952 September 25, *Kentucky Is My Land*.

1953 October 27, *The Good Spirit of Laurel Ridge*.

1954 Made poet laureate of Kentucky. October 8, suffered severe heart attack. December 23, his father died.

1955 August, Berea College awarded him the Centennial Award for Literature.

1956 November 30, *The Year of My Rebirth*.

1956 September to May, 1957, Principal of McKell High School.

1958 September 3, *Plowshare in Heaven*.

1959 Slightly condensed edition of *Man with a bull-tongue Plow* in paperback.

1960 Summer, began a year of teaching at the University of Cairo, Cairo, Egypt. August, *Huey, the Engineer* privately printed in small book form; *Jesse Stuart: A Bibliography* by Hensley C. Woodbridge published. November 5, "Jesse Stuart Room" dedicated at Murray State College. November 7, published a book on his father, *God's Oddling*.

1961 February, awarded the $5,000 Fellowship of the Academy of American Poets.

1962 May 15, *Hold April*.

1962 September 15, began good-will tour overseas for the State Department.

1963 August, *A Jesse Stuart Reader*. December 14, his three-hundredth short story "Corbie" in the *Manila Free Press*.

1964 *Save Every Lamb.*
1965 *Daughter of The Legend.*
1966 *My Land Has A Voice.*
1966 Naming and dedication of Jesse Stuart High School, Jefferson County, Kentucky.
1967 *Mr. Gallion's School.*

CHAPTER 1

The Autobiographical Writings:
Mountain Gloom and Mountain Glory

I Beyond Dark Hills

BEYOND DARK HILLS—a key book in the development of Jesse Stuart as a writer—was his first prose work to be written, but not the first to be published. Professor Edwin Mims of Vanderbilt University assigned an autobiographical paper to Stuart at precisely the right psychological moment. Stuart, a student in his Victorian poetry class, was filled with doubt and homesickness; as a result, he poured into his paper a flood of memories of his childhood, his family, and the strange vital people of the mountains. Eleven days and over three hundred typed pages later, he took the manuscript to Mims, who accepted it only after giving a grim tongue-lashing to Stuart—who was already flunking the course. A few days later Mims returned the manuscript with a hard smile and the remark—"I have been teaching school for forty years. I have never read anything so crudely written and yet beautiful, tremendous and powerful as that term paper you've written."[1] Mims, who never lost his admiration for this work, wrote in a letter several years later, "That was, of course, the most remarkable term paper I ever got from a student."[2] Stuart eventually carried the manuscript to Scotland with him and finished it in Edinburgh. In April, 1938, it was published in England by Hutchinson and in the United States by E. P. Dutton.

This story of a mountain boy's educational hegira moved an Eastern millionaire to pay for the complete college education of five young people from Stuart's community, the five recommended by Stuart.[3] The millionaire was so motivated because the motif of education is so strong in Stuart's naïve straightforward account of the first twenty-five years of his life, which might be called "The Education of Jesse Stuart." The book, episodic and anecdotal, moves forward in a loose, associative manner. It does not give a deep analysis of people but takes a quick, flashing look at them as they appear from the outside. Even the central ego, Jesse Stuart, is not deeply penetrated. What Stuart does give is a sense of vitality, of life, of human engagement which is genuine and convincing.

Stuart, who has the Scotsman's love of family and bloodline, starts his book with "Tall Figures of the Earth," six tall Scots Highland brothers who come to Virginia and eventually carry the Stuart blood to the Big Sandy River. Feuding, hard-drinking Mitch Stuart, Jesse's grandfather, begins the story melodramatically and leads us to desolate W-Hollow where Jesse is born. For twelve years Jesse moves with his family from one cabin to another, in a squatter's Odyssey which takes him over the entire valley, while vowing deeply to himself to own someday not only a house but *all* the land in the valley. We see Stuart's one-room school and the sudden glamor of Greenup High School, a beautiful place to a country boy. He fights again and again. Old Mitch Stuart is dead, but his grandson has inherited his belligerent vigor. He works hard physically and glories in his hard, muscular body. He goes to the mountain revival meetings and puzzles over the hill religion. He confronts death and tries to work out the right attitude for it—tackle it and fight it. He turns to the mountain girls and, loving them, grows dissatisfied with the drabness of mountain life. A passing carnival lures him from home for six weeks, and then he tries army life at Camp Knox.

This stint is followed by six months in the steel mills at Ashland, Kentucky, where he sees the brutality of the labor and watches a young man get disemboweled. Sickened by this accident, he works until he has paid his debts and then leaves steel for a little mountain college in Tennessee. In this fairly primitive college, Stuart works in the rock quarry and in the dining hall to support himself; but having a writer for a teacher, he begins to publish his poems in the school paper. Although he is excited by the life and the people of his college years, he returns to the Kentucky mountains, which are suddenly attractive to him again; and he teaches for a year in a little country school. He is delighted with the intelligence and vigor of his students.

Then comes a year at Vanderbilt University, where he works

as a school janitor and tries to carry a full load of graduate work. He almost kills himself, but he meets and works with such future great writers as John Crowe Ransom and Robert Penn Warren, and comes under the influence of the writer he admires most of all, Donald Davidson. The year there is in many ways a bitter one, and he finally leaves in frustration when his dormitory burns, destroying his clothing and his almost finished master's thesis on John Fox, Jr.'s fiction.

The lonesome mountain waters call him back to work through the summer on his father's farm and to start the poems which eventually become the book, *Man with a bull-tongue plow.* He commits himself to a year as county superintendent of education. This is in the worst year of the depression, and Stuart has to fight through thirty-two law suits before defeating the opposition party. Out of the nightmare year emerges his books of poems and a number of short stories. The poems and stories begin to sell; Stuart buys land, and his father builds a road from W-Hollow to the hard-topped road. It is the first time in their lives that they have been able to drive a car to their home. Jesse has won through. The book concludes as he muses poetically over vanished friends and the loves and joys that can never be repeated, over Greenup's desire to accept him now that he is a published writer, and over all his friends and family slowly submerging under the waves of time.

This bald summary cannot, of course, suggest the real appeal of the work. To do this we have to step back and look at the whole book in context with Stuart's life. This has been a popular book, and its popularity parallels that of his numerous lectures. From the first years of his life as a published writer to the present time, he has been much sought after as a lecturer. There seems no doubt that his many audiences have been as delighted by the *substance* of his talks as by his vigorous, masculine delivery. Stuart's life seems inherently fascinating, and in a sense all of his work—novels, short stories, poems, autobiographies— has been a prolonged, public exploration of the varied facets of that life. Certain mythic patterns or archetypes emerge in *Beyond Dark Hills* to provide a kind of secondary structure for the book.

We get an inkling of this if we categorize *Beyond Dark Hills* as an autobiography and then add that it has a strong pastoral flavor. It also has a kind of Horatio Algeresque *Bound-To-Rise* character to it. These familiar mythic patterns are still moving ones. Our protagonist, Jesse Stuart, is in one sense the innocent abroad in a vexed and complex world. When Stuart is away at college, he looks back on his mountain home; and it takes on Edenic characteristics—the garden in which his mother works in the fresh May morning, the lavish supply of delicious food, the hill beauty of spring, bright with dogwood and redbud. Like Antaeus, he returns to the mountains to renew his strength from the earth; his body draws strength from the hard labor in the soil; his mind, peace from the solitude and beauty of the mountains. His imagination is moved to poetry and creation by the cycle of nature through the mountain seasons, and he becomes a successful writer *not* by going to New York, but by returning to the mountains where he can be close to the earth. He is a country boy who goes out into the world and becomes a success, not by selling out to the city but by returning to the country. This pastoral Horatio Alger hero fascinates and delights a contemporary audience, as if it gratifies some secret desire in the reader which he cannot openly espouse. Undoubtedly, there is a kind of modern Thoreauvian appeal to *Beyond Dark Hills.*

We might consider the structural pattern of the book from a different angle by pointing out that there are three major themes running through the book that tie together the episodes in Stuart's life: ambivalence, primitivism, and education. In the theme dealing with ambivalence, Stuart displays an early dislike of the hills and of his father which later turns to love and affection. As he remembers it, this hate began in 1918 with the death of an infant brother from pneumonia, the second brother to die from this disease. The family buried the boy on the farm of Stuart's grandfather. It was a traumatic experience for Stuart. A heavy snow fell in April, 1918. Stuart was walking to the barn with his father. He refused to step in his father's tracks as he had done before when the deep snows came. He vowed in his mind to leave and repudiate both the hills and the father. His brothers were dead, he felt, because his father had stayed in these hills where it was impossible to get a doctor to treat them. Until this incident he had admired his father and identified with him. Refusing to step in his father's footsteps, he dramatizes for himself and for us an identity crisis that runs through the book and gives it much of its inner form. He makes his decision: "Now these hills will not always hold me. I shall go beyond them some day."[4] They seem heavy and oppressive; they enclose him.

But the incomparable mountain spring brought a healing to Stuart that he never forgot. He came to love the physical beauty and exuberance of the mountain life, and things quieted down inside him until his high school years came to an end. Then ". . . things to me were not what they once were. I dreamed of something beyond the hills. I wanted to go and go and go. I wanted to do something. One night I was sitting in the chipyard talking to my father. I told him fifty acres of land was not a big enough place for me. He sat silently and gazed at a bunch of hollyhocks in the moonlight" (p. 71). High school ended, and young Stuart longed for gay clothes, parties, romance, escape from the drab hills. "My whole life was empty. I hated the hills. I had a desire to leave and never return. . . . I said to myself: 'You ought to see me, Pa: I'm leaving here sometime today. My life is too empty here. I can stand it no longer'" (p. 109). So he burned all his books, in a dramatic gesture of repudiation, then slipped in to bid his mother good-bye, but left without trying to see his father. This angered Mitch, who sent word for Jesse to stay away. Jesse vowed to stay away until his father sent for him.

He did stay away for a year; but, when Christmas came, he longed for home. He hitch-hiked back and was received like the prodigal son. His father, delighted to see him again, took him over the farm and showed him the cribs and improvements. Jesse saw deeper lines on his father's face, and realized how much hard work and exposure had broken him. A new respect and love came to him for this tough, sinewy little man. He went back to college and finished his degree; and suddenly, longing for his own hills, he returned in the marvelous hill May: "Home was good to see again. My folks were glad to see me there . . . . Here was the life I liked. I knew it. But I kept it to myself. I didn't want people to know how much I had loved the hills and how much I had hated them. It took life beyond these hills to make one love life among the hills. . . . I found it sour when I went beyond. . . . It was not sweet like the life in the hills" (p. 226). The pendulum is swinging and his love grows for what he has earlier hated. The curve of the book leads Jesse closer and closer to his father. Scene after scene gives us this new amity between father and son. Jesse rushed in one day to show his amazed father a check for one hundred and twenty-five dollars received for a short story. "God Almighty, Jess . . . I didn't know you was that sharp after the way you bumfuzzled the Superintendent's office. I'd have to work two month's to get that, beatin' it out on the railroad. You stay in the smokehouse if you can do that. I'll hoe the corn" (p. 388).

Then the father made a statement he had never made before: "I've come in a one having a lot of fights over you when you was Superintendent. Old Dan Manburn tried to pop off about you. I told him to shut his damn trap or I'd smash it. I says: '. . . He's my boy and you can't talk about him like that in my presence'" (p. 388). Jesse moved closer and closer to his father and defended him against his brother James's attack: "I used to despise my father. Refused to step in his tracks in the snow. Now I wonder if I'm worthy!" (p. 392). Jesse records his fathers' delight on seeing the first copy of *Man with a bull-tongue plow.* "I never thought you had a book in your head. I want you to read that book to me sometime when we're not so busy with the work" (p. 393). Then at the very end of the book comes the climax: Jesse's father, after a lifetime of desiring a road out from their land, builds the road with his own labor and the first car in family history drives up before the Stuart house. The father says: "Son, get in that car and take me over the road I built out of this hollow. Take me to town. I just want to ride around the hills these ol' legs has clim' ten thousand times over. I want a glass of beer and a cigar anyway" (p. 395).

It is clear that by the time Stuart has returned from Vanderbilt University and made his strategic decision to give himself to the land that this ambivalence is being resolved. The realization that his father is an unusual and, in many ways, heroic person begins in *Beyond Dark Hills* and expands into his later book *God's Oddling,* which clearly shows his mature *love* for his father. His ambivalence toward the mountains is resolved also into a love for them which does not overlook the real cruelties and brutalities implicit in much of the mountain life.

This love for the mountains becomes the theme of primitivism, mentioned above as one of the unifying themes of this book, as it is of virtually all of his books. For centuries the primitivist has told us that life close to the soil is the good life, that man finds happiness by following the norms of nature. Stuart, who goes along with this doctrine unequivocally, affirms it in an apostrophe to Bill Ludlow, a mountain bootlegger who is being carted off to jail: ". . . Bill Ludlow, don't leave the soil. Live right down against the soil. Be envious of the snake because it rubs the soil closer than you. . . . from the bitterness of life among the hills, there is the greatest sweetness in the world. . . . There is a beauty in the soil that is unsurpassed. . . . 'The heavens declare the Glory of God.' . . . I never knew what it meant until I got away from it" (pp. 260-61).

Not the least of the attractions of the land is the freedom it gives. This point is plainly made when Jesse asks his father and mother to move into town, where life will be easier for them: "Let me tell you something. . . . I aim to stay right here. I aim to give this farm to you two boys before I drop off. And I want you to carry on. . . . This is a place where you can do as you please and there is not a boss to look down your collar and watch you sweat. . . . And you see that little knoll up there where that hickory stands, I want to be buried there. I want your ma to be buried there beside me. . . . I want us to be up high, overlooking this farm and above the cornfields, the strawberries and the tobacco fields. . . . Now you see this is done. . . . And I want you to carry on" (p. 280).

As with so many primitivisms of the past, there is in Stuart's primitivism a bit of anti-intellectualism and a bit of a God-in-nature mystique. This combination appears clearly as he sits in the courtyard on county-court day in Greenup and watches the hill people dance to the old-time fiddlers. As he watches, he thinks back over his work at Lincoln Memorial and his graduate work at Vanderbilt: "'If getting educated makes me hate old-time music and old mountain ballads, then I'm not getting along very well with my education.' I could never lose my love and appreciation for them. I didn't want to. The mountain people are the happiest people in the world. Go off to college and get educated and lose appreciation for things you loved before you went away. . . . Get educated so that you can know God—Oh, my heavens, how foolish! I cry out against it all. . . . It's foolish to get educated to know God. Get close to the soil and know Him. Get educated and forget life. That's what you'll do if you're not careful" (p. 296).

It seems clear then that Stuart's primitivism is a natural attitude—one growing out of his way of life. It is *not* a romantic escape from life, inculcated by reading Rousseauesque books on the delights of untrammeled nature. For Stuart is about as honest a primitivist as we can find in our country today; he knows as well as any writer living the grimness and tragedy of life on the mountain soil. When he chose it as a way of life, he was choosing something he knew. The Agrarians at Vanderbilt University talked and wrote much of the joy of life on the farm, but they took university appointments and kept to the life of the libraries and classrooms. We can say of Stuart that he *practiced* what *they* preached.

Education, the third major theme running through the book, is discussed at greater length in the section devoted to Stuart's *Thread That Runs So True*. Suffice it to say here that the point he makes again and again about education in *Beyond Dark Hills* is that the excellence of the individual teacher is the key to learning, whether it is his high school English teacher, or Harry Kroll at Lincoln Memorial, or Donald Davidson at Vanderbilt—three teachers who greatly influenced him.

Aside from the thematic motifs discussed above, some mention should be made of the writing technique in the present book. An early book, it shows some immaturities of style. The writer sounds, for instance, more like Aldous Huxley than Jesse Stuart when he looks at a rundown schoolhouse with bats, spiders, and rats in it, with weeds overgrowing the yard, and remarks—"It was all very amusing" (p. 262). Eliot's *Waste Land* was much in vogue when *Beyond Dark Hills* was written, and Stuart cannot resist a too arty reference to ". . . rat prints. They will smooth them over and the rats will make them again. And thus it happens in the waste land. They are the symbols of the desolation, you see" (p. 252). This imitative strain is the temptation of every young writer and Stuart falls—but not very often.

Happily, the Huxleyan echoes noted above are more than drowned out by the idiom of the country. "Faze" is authentic, as in, " 'Now, how air you going to faze him tonight?' 'I'll faze him. You give me two hoots of corn licker' " (p. 247). Jesse's father speaks in this manner about their dog, old Black-Boy: "That old dog has been a great dog. If he'd a-been a man he'd a-been the Governor of Kentucky. But now he is only an old dog and he is very tired. He ain't much longer for here" (p. 273). It is a delight to hear the idiom of that last sentence. From the Ashland steel mills we hear the following monologue: "We got to weed-monkeying together. We took my Chivy roadster, a couple of blankets, and a little licker and how we did get them. But we got a whole lot of them rotten stinking kind. And God, when one of them *weedmonkeys* smells she's enough to vomit a buzzard" (p. 163). A "weedmonkey" is a cheap whore who plies her trade in the weeds or bushes.

This earthy idiom of the hill country blends well with the rich folk material scattered throughout the book. Stuart's folk background is completely natural and unforced, and thus far more convincing to the reader than that of an antiquarian or self-conscious collector of folk materials. It wells up in his impressionistic description of a Labor Day celebration in Greenup. The farm people swarm in from the country and dance in the street. The old time fiddlers play songs like "Sourwood Mountain," "The Hangman's Song," "The Little Mohee," "Loving Nancy," and a song which begins: "In London far city a lady did dwell, / Concerning her beauty no tongue can tell." They play the old games—climb a greased pole, run a sack race and a wheelbarrow race, have hog-calling and cow-calling contests. Liquor flows and everybody is happy. A young mountain couple gets married, and the young males surround the house on the wedding night beating cow-bells, plow-points, and dish-pans; blowing fox-horns; and firing shotguns until all their shells are gone. They call this "Bellin' the Bride." Or when a mountain woman dies and is buried in a home-made coffin which is carried in a wagon to a wintry mountain top, the women stand by her grave and sing "There's a Land Beyond the River."

For the most part, the folk enter the narrative in an exuberant, straightforward fashion. At times they are the bearer of Stuart's irony, as in his description of Brother Hammertight, the Holy-Roller preacher, and his guitar-playing girls who sing a holiness hymn, "I Would Not Be Denied." Stuart then describes a Dionysian scene in which all the worshippers become drunk on religious emotion, wallow and shout and jump in a very ecstasy, and confess their sins to the discomfiture of some of their fellow worshippers. One sinner drops to her knees and prays: " 'God have mercy on me. I slept with Jake Hicks. God don't let my man hurt Jake.' Jake Hicks . . . leaves the house. He says when he goes out of the door: 'You can't fool with women. They'll tell every time. I'm in a hell of a fix. Damn old Holy Rollers anyhow' " (p. 245). Brother Hammertight, who continues to dance and shout, climbs the stovepipe until it falls. One man cuts

Brother Hammertight's suspenders, and he dances out of his trousers; the women flee shouting, and he dances outdoors off into the darkness under the tall beech trees. Through the night the men and women disperse up the mountain trails singing thinly

I would not be denied
I would not be denied
Since Jesus come and saved my soul
I would not be denied.

Stuart's laughter follows them up the trails, but he is laughing both with them and at them.

In this book, Stuart obviously abandons the conventional autobiographical form in favor of a loose impressionistic structure which jumps from personal experience to meditation, and from meditation to long quotations from quaint Kentucky characters; occasionally, he intersperses the narrative with his own poems. Part autobiography, part family chronicle, part a lyric celebration of the beauty and gloom of mountain life, the book is loosely episodic, following the general drift of Stuart's life. It moves forward jerkily but with a kind of speed to it. The characters are portrayed only because they serve to dramatize certain phases of Stuart's life. We get brief intriguing glimpses of these people; we would like to see more of them.

As a result the best chapters in the book (the chapters on the hill religion, the steel mill, Stuart's year as a school superintendent) never realize the artistic potential of fully developed episodes. Occasionally the writing is self-consciously rhetorical. When we have made these reservations, we still have left an absorbing book with a kind of Adam and Eve freshness about it, and with a masculinity that delights the reader. It shows us the reasons for "mountain gloom and mountain glory," and it makes us live through them. After thirty years it still rings true. Chances are it will continue to do so.

II The Thread That Runs So True

For years—since 1937, in fact—a book had been tumbling over and over in Stuart's head. More than anything else he wanted to write a book about teaching—a book that would be a song, a poem, a manifesto, a hymn to the profession of teaching. Stuart is a passionate man, a kind of literary karate expert in the sense that all of his being—mind, heart, soul—converges to a point in every narrative blow; he throws himself completely into a book and holds back nothing.

In 1940, Dr. Clarence Poe, editor of *The Progressive Farmer,* asked Stuart to do an article about teaching that would help the South hold some of its emigrating teachers. "When I got his letter, I realized what I had to say was more than an article. First I tried to put it into fiction. The wind blew some of the pages away from my writing room, scattered them over the yard. I found only part of them. I regarded this as a bad omen, a wrong way to start the book, so I changed to personal experience and the truth—no exaggerations. In 1948, late, I had it finished."[5]

When *The Thread That Runs So True* was published in 1949, reviewers sensed immediately the impact this work would have on teachers. Reviews in newspapers all across the country seconded the praise of Dr. Jay Elmer Morgan, founder and president of the National Education Association, who wrote ". . . *The Thread That Runs So True* is the best book on education written in the last fifty years."[6] One of the remarkable things about this book is the fact that it began with a good sale and has continually increased its sale each year. Its readers have mailed thousands and thousands of letters to Stuart. Even today his mail carries eight to ten letters a day from people who are ignited by his interest in teaching. In an age of the shoddy, uninterested and corrupt worker, it is a revivifying experience to meet in the pages of a book a teacher who really did walk a twenty-mile round trip to carry a suitcase full of books to his print-hungry students in a country school. This immense conviction of Stuart's, his sturdy sincerity, and his cyclonic energy hit the reader like an electric shock and account for the wide and enduring appeal of this book in an age surfeited with cynicism and despair.

The actual story is Stuart's own life as a teacher, related episodically with a few names altered to keep from offending living persons. Structurally, the episodes are clustered about an old play-song, "The Thread That Runs So True," sung by the mountain children in Stuart's childhood and young manhood:

> The needle's eye that does supply,
> The thread that runs so true,
> Many a beau, have I let go
> Because I wanted you.

Many a dark and stormy night,
When I went home with you,
I stumped my toe and down I go,
Because I wanted you.

Each of the six parts of the book takes its title from a line, or an altered version of a line from the play-song. Part I, "The Needle's Eye That Does Supply," begins with Stuart, a boy just seventeen years old, starting his first day of teaching. He has picked a one-room school in Lonesome Valley because his sister had taught here, been beaten up and run off by the school bully, Guy Hawkins. Guy traps Stuart in school alone and forces him into a vicious fight which Stuart wins with a flying tackle. This fight is the literal and symbolic beginning of a long teaching career which involved Stuart in many different kinds of fights—verbal, legal, and physical. It also established him solidly in a community that respected physical prowess above all.

The teacher finds immediately that there is no monotony in his life. Dressed in a handsome white suit, he starts through the balmy night to pay court to beautiful May Woods, the bonny teacher of Upper Lonesome School. From a dark woods, a sudden barrage of rotten tomatoes, eggs, melons, and squash rains down on him bespattering his trim suit—and ending his courting.

He teaches the mountain children how to make paper cups and drink in a sanitary fashion. He tracks down a boy who has been drawing obscene pictures in the latrine. He spanks a beautiful fourteen-year-old girl who has been covertly spitting tobacco juice on the freshly painted walls of the school house. Her father, who happens to be both Stuart's landlord and a school trustee, turns on the teacher and forces him to move to a new house. Most important of all, the teacher, trying to teach eight grades in one room, hits on the technique of couching each recitation in the form of a game. When the whole school devotes itself with joy to the process of learning, the teacher has mastered his most important technique. Even the former bully, Guy Hawkins, is swept into the school's enthusiasm. Lonesome Valley School challenges Upper Lonesome School to an arithmetic contest, and wins when Margaret Prater turns down seven of the best students from Upper Lonesome. Stuart ends his six-month term by promoting twenty-year-old Guy Hawkins from the first to the fifth grade; and he is a little sad to leave the countryside where he has spent the most exciting months of his life. Teaching fascinates him.

Part II, "The Thread That Runs So True," begins with a summation of the next five years of Stuart's life, the years that cover his work in a steel mill and his college period. He returns home with a college degree, determined *not* to teach; but his parents urge him to take a teaching job and he does. He becomes the principal and entire faculty of little Winston High, which lies seventeen miles from the county seat on a dirt road impassable to autos from November to May. His school building is a one-room tumbled down ex-lodge hall, but he has fourteen bright students to work with, capped by Budge Waters, an authentic scholastic genius. The teacher, who has to teach five subjects—algebra, Latin, plane geometry, history, and English—has trouble keeping ahead of his students; but his love for them is proved by his long walking trips home to carry books back to them. They love him for it, and he becomes a friend of all of these land-locked Anglo-Saxon families, whose blood has been in this valley for one hundred and fifty years. Stuart joins them in their recreation—their hunting, fishing, sorghum parties, and dances. As he stands on the mountain wall one day, he decides that if *each* teacher in America would inspire his students, all would then be well with America for the teacher held the destiny of a great country in his hand and all other professions stemmed from the teaching profession.

Then one zero day he starts walking the seventeen miles home in a blizzard. Night falls; he loses his way and is forced to spend the night in an open field in twelve below zero temperature, but is almost miraculously saved from freezing to death by discovering shocks of fodder and pulling them over him to keep him warm. Two days later he walks seventeen miles back to Winston with a suitcase of books for his students. The bitter zero wind freezes his hands and feet to a dangerous numbness. The students repay this monumental devotion by riding mule-back seventeen miles through the snow to challenge and defeat large Landsburgh High in a scholastic contest. Budge Waters, the genius, carries off first places in English literature, grammar, history, and civil government. Great is the rejoicing back in Tiber Valley when the word spreads that tiny Winston has won a David-like victory over Goliath Landsburgh. When Budge Waters enters the state contests, he wins two first places, history and grammar. Stuart is borne up as on the wings of eagles through the valley— he has a great reputation as a teacher. When the Landsburgh City School Board offers him a position as principal of Landsburgh High, he accepts.

Part III, "I Stumped My Toe And Down I Go," takes Stuart through his period as principal of Landsburgh High, where his first shock comes when he learns that his salary is one hundred and eleven dollars a month for nine months, exactly what his teachers make. But he has a young and ambitious faculty and a school so crowded that one class must be scheduled in a hall; so he throws all of his energy and vigor into running a reasonably tight ship. He mediates feuds on the football team, learns that the sulphur on weeds has turned his trouser legs green to the gossipy delight of the townspeople, takes an upstairs room in the hotel and sees at night the town's favorite bootlegger selling, from his long topcoat, liquor to adults and high school students alike; and he reads freshmen themes which have some of the wild poetry of John Millington Synge's *Riders To The Sea.*

The school year quickly runs to its end in May. Stuart attends a great school fair and meets Nancy Cochran, whom he had known as a pretty young girl at Lonesome Valley. She is now married, has five children, and brings him nostalgic news about how things have changed in Lonesome Valley where he had first taught school. The Landsburgh school board meets and refuses to rehire Stuart; he had asked too much money for salary. He walks away, anxious to try something new.

Part IV, "Many a Dark And Stormy Night," begins with a quick two-page summary of Stuart's year of graduate study at Vanderbilt. After it he accepts an appointment as Superintendent of the county schools, the highest office in the county educational system. Immediately trouble arises: A feud begins with the city schools, and one erupts in the school board itself. Lawsuits—ultimately totaling thirty-two—begin and are fought to a bitter finish. Stuart wins, he says, thirty-one and a half. He sets out on a tour of eighty-two county schools and visits everyone, including a mountain school so high up that in bad weather the school "marm" has to be pushed up the steep slope by the students and then lowered by rope. He dates one of his beautiful mountain school teachers one night and runs a gauntlet of pistol bullets to his sister's home—the local boys don't like outsiders who date their girls. He ends the tour with a vision of consolidated schools which will replace these one-room affairs and with a completely fatigued car which is sold as scrap for twenty-five dollars.

The school board raises him to one hundred and twenty-five dollars a month, and he gets one check of his new salary before the banks go broke. (Five years later he is paid the remainder of his salary.) He works the rest of the year, as do his teachers, without pay. He develops a great admiration for his teachers and their profession, but he longs to reform the conditions under which they work. He writes articles attacking the trustee system, but no one will print them. He completes a cycle of sonnets and reads selections to Naomi Deane, his fiancée. The school year closes, he burns his controversial manuscripts, resigns his position, and recommends himself as principal of Maxwell High School.

In Part V, "Many A School Have I Let Go," Stuart chronicles his four years at Maxwell High, good years during which his experiments in education were carried forward and during which he begins a lecture career that was to extend into thirty years and thousands of lectures covering the United States, the Near East, and the Far East—some forty-odd countries in all.

Maxwell High was a clean well-arranged school with spacious grounds. Stuart immediately sets about improving education. He publishes an invitation for all county teachers who have never finished high school to enroll at Maxwell High. Many do, and he finds the ages of his students ranging from eleven to sixty-nine years of age. The older teacher-students blend in well; they help stabilize the student body and frequently serve as substitute teachers. He discovers a young girl, Eustacia Pratt, who, she says, never makes mistakes. She becomes his secretary and the protagonist of a short story, "Eustacia," the money from which pays her way through college. She in turn helps her two sisters through college.

For a while hoodlums threaten all of Maxwell High's public entertainment. When the law fails to protect him, Stuart whips one of the loafers so badly that the threat is ended for good. He sees the late legislature abolish the trustee system and establish tenure for teachers, reforms he has long fought for. During a two-day snow storm, he turns out three short stories and sells them all immediately—a real turning point in his life. The money from the stories gives him the first surplus money he has ever had—and he discovers for the first time the difference between a savings and a checking account. All teachers in Kentucky he says, have to have a sideline to keep them alive. Writing will be *his*.

When Eastern State Teachers College invites him to deliver a convocation lecture, Stuart is a howling, uproarious success. Scheduled to lecture for thirty minutes, he finds his audience won't allow him to stop. Eighty-seven minutes later he quits while the audience stands, applauds, and laughs. Stuart finds he is a natural humorist. He said the most serious things in what he hoped were the most serious tones, and his audience roared with laughter. This quality he shares with his great literary predecessor, Mark Twain. The fame of his talk and his book of poetry, *Man with a bull-tongue Plow*, spreads; and he find himself on the lecture circuit, traveling from Princeton to upper Michigan to the lower Southern states. On these university campuses Stuart searches out and finds scholarships for thirty-seven young men and women of his mountain county. When Lee Shuttuck of Boston read *Beyond Dark Hills*, he provided five scholarships for Stuart's mountain students.

In April the young author receives a note that he has won a Guggenheim Fellowship for study abroad. He receives a year's leave of absence.

Part VI, "Because I Wanted You," is the concluding movement of the book. Stuart returns from Europe to find he has no job because a new and repressive administration has taken over the county school system. Stuart fights back, establishing his own newspaper to do so. His life is threatened, and his family push him into a job at a large, fine high school in Dartmouth, Ohio. When he returns to his home town one weekend, he is black-jacked and severely injured by an enemy who is later fined two-hundred dollars in a court trial. Suddenly there is a great exodus of teachers from Kentucky and from Greenup County. Stuart blames the miserable, hypocritical, short-sighted politicians and decides to quit teaching. He quits, and begins to farm and raise sheep; on October 14, 1939, he marries Naomi Deane Norris, whom he had courted for seventeen years.

Such is the substance of the narrative. Within this structure certain thematic bones do stand out. There is the horrifying fact, documented over and over again, that at the time Stuart wrote,

Kentucky was an educational wasteland. Underpaid, overworked, lacking tenure, the teachers knew themselves to be viciously exploited. In spite of this situation, the miracle was that Kentucky still had scattered about in its schools great teachers like Jesse Stuart. And they stayed in such an educational hovel because they, like Stuart, felt the enormous potential of the students who were there, who looked to them for intellectual food.

This absolute need of the mountain students for education is another theme that is prominent in the narrative. Stuart sees the children walking barefooted to school, leaving blood on the frost-hard ground. He sees a scholastic genius like Budge Waters walking seven miles in order to attend a *one*-teacher high school. The need was there in the 1930's and 1940's, and Stuart reacted to it by making learning a kind of play. Pedagogues may disagree about his techniques, but there is no doubt that his students found his classes gay and competitive. They enjoyed getting into the game—for such it seemed to them. They would do anything for a teacher who would risk his life for them—which he did. Wherever he taught, from a one-room mountain school to huge Dartmouth High School, he brought a quickening air to things of the mind. He particularized them to the point of a direct contact between him and the student.

There is, throughout the book, Stuart's immense love and respect for the individual. Emerson had long been a familiar of his, and he carries Emerson's respect for the individual into his teaching of his mountain students. Emerson's "Self-Reliance" shows in Stuart's celebration of the will. In a sense, his entire book is a long hymn to the human will. The protagonist is confronted by a series of seemingly insuperable obstacles, but he hurls himself against each and gradually wins every battle, and is still alive at the end of the book, still fighting on. One phase of this struggle is the group of teaching problems he encounters, beginning with the problems of Guy Hawkins, of painting the school, of teaching fifty-four classes in one day, and of what to do about the trustee system. One of the great fascinations of the book lies in the pleasure the reader takes in the pragmatic solutions of the young teacher.

The real problem of mass education in the United States today is how to get a *good* teacher into each classroom. If the United States could put a Jesse Stuart in each classroom, it would solve its problem. The ironic thing—dangerous and portentous too for the future of our educational system—is that the system, instead of recognizing the value of this selfless, dynamic, and creative teacher, rejected him. After nine years of teaching Stuart found he had averaged one hundred dollars and thirty cents a month. He wanted to marry, but two people could not live on that. He faced his fiancée and said: "Teaching is not charitable work. It is a profession. It is the greatest profession under the sun. I don't know of any profession that is more important to the people upon this earth. I've loved it. I still love it. But I'm leaving it because it's left me."[7]

Certainly in terms of form the book passes the pragmatic test. Stuart wrote it so well that twenty years after its publication it is selling twenty-five thousand copies a year and increasing its sales each year. A book that has such success without resorting to the lures of sex and sensationalism has the right innate form, and the essence of his form is the dramatic. Whatever Stuart wishes to tell, he dramatizes. The first page pitches us into the conflict with Guy Hawkins, and from this point the book spins breathlessly through a series of short, kinetic episodes spanning ten years in Stuart's teaching life and reaching its climax in his marriage to Naomi Norris.

The style is simple and direct, with strong sensory images and a good sprinkling of metaphors. The use of single-line excerpts from the play song, "The Needle's Eye," as thematic titles for the six sections is a striking and poetic way of pointing up the structural unity of the book. For the sake of drama, Stuart introduces strong contrasts into the book. Good and evil are sharply divided—there are no gray areas of overlap. Stuart confronts "Bad John Bledsoe" who has come to his office to collect a debt or take it out of Stuart's skin. Bad John is no ordinary antagonist; he is almost a fairy-tale ogre, six feet something and tipping the scale at 296 pounds of coal-heaver muscles. The book is replete with such physical encounters between titans who battle with saga-like ferocity.

Yet this is no "never-never land." Stuart's firsthand knowledge validates every page. The saga quality derives from the fact that Stuart is a man who is cast in a heroic mold—both physically and spiritually. He resists physical aggression as he does spiritual and legal aggression—heroically and absolutely. The saga quality derives also from the extreme simplicity of his native county: Life there is primitive and direct. Reading about it reminds one of Ireland in 1900, of Maurice Sullivan's *Twenty Years A'Grow-ing*, of Synge's *Riders to the Sea* and *Playboy of the Western World*, and of Sean O'Faolain's short stories. Such a primitive land is a land fit for sagas and for heroes. Everything—problems, solutions, heroes, villains—all seem bigger than life, transmuted by Stuart's artistry, yet clearly tied back to life. And the book soon had its affect on real life.

Certainly the vast concern America felt over its schools in the 1950's and 1960's derived in part from this spirit-awakener. If any one man sounded the tocsin, Stuart did. From complex and ambivalent studies of educational problems and trends, we turn with relief to this clear-eyed, youthful testament of faith in edu- cation—faith despite crucifixions.

III The Year of My Rebirth

There came a day in the fall of 1954 when Jesse Stuart stood before a huge audience in Murray State College Auditorium. A chartered plane waited to whisk him from Murray to Flora, Illinois, where he would give another major talk in the afternoon. He stood there a dynamic two-hundred-twenty pounder, strong as a professional fullback. He talked a full hour to the standing-room-only audience and rushed out to catch his ride to his plane. He never caught it. He stumbled and fell to the ground—struck down by a massive coronary. But, as his brain faded into darkness, he kept saying to himself—*I will not die, I will not die.* The doctor told Mrs. Stuart that there were only three chances in a thousand that he would live, but his enormous will saved him. It took him a full year to come back to a nearly normal life, and *The Year of My Rebirth* is the story of that year.

This book is difficult to place, for it is many things in one. First of all, it is a journal of one year in the life of the author; second, it is a spiritual autobiography; third, a collection of personal essays, of sketches, and occasionally of prose poems. Stuart began writing the book as a kind of therapy—he needed the physical act of writing to recover the muscular agility of his fingers and hand, and the mental concentration to counteract the feeling of insecurity and melancholy that at times overwhelmed him. The reader following the month-by-month account of Stuart's gradual return to life has an odd kind of empathy with Stuart. He sees

that Stuart at the beginning of his convalescence fumbles un-
easily and unsteadily about. Then, as his strength and confidence
gradually return, he moves more alertly and surely. He is reborn
in the sense of coming anew to the physical world and learning
to walk again as an infant would, and in the spiritual sense of
passing from death to life and feeling a fresh sense of the reality
of God and of God's universe.

Stuart gives us a prologue to the actual body of the journal, a
prologue which sets up the predisposing conditions of his heart
attack. As a boy, he had lived in a time-free world with two
dogs, plenty of food and outdoor work and play; as a result he
had tremendous strength and power, and no tensions. When success as a writer and lecturer arrived, he became a man on the
run, giving in one year eighty-nine talks in thirty-nine states,
besides publishing two books and numerous articles, short stories,
and poems. He found that the only time he now had to write
poems was in airports and in railway and bus stations. He became a schedule man, searching out tiny gaps in his routine into
which he could jam still other duties.

He saw three men pitch forward on the streets and die of
heart attacks, but he knew this couldn't happen to him. When
his wife warned him he was doing too much, he laughed and
worked faster. He was still as strong as any man in the county;
he could pick up a three hundred pound sack of cement and
carry it across the garage floor. He took on more talks and got a
pain in his chest that would not go away. A heart specialist, who
worked two days on him, finally told him not to worry; the pain
was purely muscular. Two weeks later he collapsed completely
at Murray with a massive coronary. Then came the hospital,
oxygen tent, a constant stream of nurses and doctors, dreams
and hallucinations, impulses of despair and suicide, and gradually
the upturn. The crisis passed and late in November Stuart began
his journey home, taking six days to make the five hundred mile
trip. He was completely fatigued. But he gradually began his
convalescence; and on January 1, 1955, he began his journal.
From January to December, 1955, the great cycle of the months
went rolling forward, and Stuart grew gradually back to the full
life he had once known.

The flavor of this book can best be conveyed by showing the
motifs which recur most frequently throughout the book: namely,
W-Hollow as "place," the cycle of the seasons, home town as joy

[36]

and agony, death, and the centrality of his father to Stuart's life.

At first he can only walk to the window and look out on the hills and hollows of W-Hollow and watch the ever changing weather. But he feels the importance of this as "place" to him. Then comes a day when he can walk out into the yard for the first time, and the wind bright as polished silver rushes over him; he rests his hand on the rough bark of a dogwood tree and is overwhelmed by winter's dark beauty. Gradually he walks farther each day down the road, one day passing beyond the sight of the house but staying in the middle of the road so that if he falls with an attack he can easily be found. He grows stronger and finally walks a mile with a deep sense of triumph. He goes under shade trees and naps; he watches the fresh green of spring, the white of percoon blossoms appear; and he repossesses his entire valley, content to let the outside world fade and to become one once again with his valley. In March a fire, driven by the gusty winds, races through Stuart's trees and the underbrush to threaten his barns and house. His relatives and friends finally beat it out, while Stuart the invalid stands impotently by, unable to fight this enemy of his valley.

Stuart has a deep, personalized love for this valley and his meditations go to it again and again. He broods over its history and is struck by the cyclical character of the immigration into the valley. The Byrnes came first to W-Hollow and settled it in 1800, but by 1850 the family had all died. About 1850 the Daughertys came, and loved and worked the land for half a century, but by 1900 the last male descendant had died. Then the Stuarts appeared in 1900 and began to work the land, raising hay, cattle, sorghum cane, tobacco, some sweet potatoes, and strawberries. Stuart's tone grows more elegiac as he foresees the end of his own line: "The Stuarts still remain, but I am the last, and have no sons. It is a half-century valley for any one family, and our time is about up."[8] And Stuart himself never left W-Hollow because, "I cannot desert what has made me. I tell people there's something in the land that won't let me leave and that I am nothing without the land. This is the truest answer I know" (p. 265).

Stuart has a fancy for food direct from the earth. When April brings the first green to W-Hollow, he writes a dissertation on savory "hodgepodge" greens. Naomi Stuart, who goes about the yard collecting the ingredients, picked Willie britches (also called

Whitetop), narrow dock, young plantain, Johnny-jump-ups, pepper grass, wild beet, Sweet Annie, tender young poke, pig ear, some rare ruffled lettuce, and more of the slick and common lettuce. All of these are washed thoroughly, cooked together, and served with fried bacon and hot corn bread. When Stuart ate this dish in early April, he felt the strength of the earth pour back into him.

July brings golden-rod back to W-Hollow, and Stuart thinks nostalgically of the long trek he made through Scotland, retracing the steps of Robert Burns from town to town until he came to Burns's mausoleum at St. Michael's. He returned at night in the bright moonlight, and stood by the tomb of the man whose poetry had changed his entire life by inspiring him to be a poet. Taking from a volume of Burns's poetry a sprig of pressed golden-rod which he had carried all the way from W-Hollow, he dropped this golden-rod on Burns's grave to pay his tribute to the poet of Scottish earth.

Christmas draws near, and Stuart records one night when he and his wife and their daughter Jane sit by the open wood fire in their kitchen grate and roast apples, pop corn, and crack and pick hickory nuts for a cake. Then they sing Christmas carols and ten year old Jane recites "The Night Before Christmas." After his wife and daughter go to bed, Stuart closes the door and sits alone in the kitchen warmed by the fires of the grate and of family love. His mind dreams back over his childhood days, the supper times of his youth spent in this same valley and on this very spot, because Stuart had his new kitchen built on the same spot of earth that his father's kitchen had rested on. He feels the currents of the past flowing into his mind and merging with the warm familiar love which still floats palpably in the air of the fire-lit kitchen. As the year wanes, his family memories and the reality of W-Hollow merge. He is devoted to "place," and for him W-Hollow is *the place*. Memory begins for him here, and Plum Grove Churchyard in the heart of the valley will receive him in death.

Interwoven with the W-Hollow motif is Stuart's fascination with the seasons. Ever and ever his eye turns to the sky and the clouds, to the weather of W-Hollow, to the new green of the earth, to the awakening terrapins of the spring, to the August fields of ripening tobacco, to the falling oak leaves of fall, to the dark, grim beauty of the snow-covered hills.

Spring comes to W-Hollow with April, and in April Stuart's heart leaps up as at no other season of the year. This year more than ever, April reminds him of the resurrection theme. "Reborn myself, I shall watch more carefully the rebirth going on all around me" (p. 74). "I like to think I can put my ear down against the earth and hear the noises of growing roots" (p. 73). Bright waters fall from the cliff, sun-silvered. The clean winds of April bring him the first faint smell of new vegetation—it has a healing, annealing effect and seems to strengthen his damaged heart. "Hold April," he says, "never let it go."

Again and again in April the Resurrection theme rises in his mind.

How can any farmer ever doubt resurrection? . . . There was never a time when I doubted the resurrection of Christ. . . . The man who has never planted a seed would be the first to doubt the story of the resurrection. . . . Maybe this is the reason there are so many believers in resurrection among farmers and people who live on the land, who keep their feet on the ground and their eyes on the stars. . . . There are more true poets where people plow the land, work with animals under the sun and stars, feel the rain and wind in God's world, than there are in city apartments. . . . Where God is Scientist, I see resurrection with my own eyes. I feel confident—I have faith—that when man, the seed of God, is planted in the ground, though his husk will go back to the earth, he will be resurrected into a new life, for this is the law of God (p. 84-6).

There is no doubt that Stuart's heart attack, bringing him to the very edge of the black country of death, greatly increased his consciousness of the resurrection motif in nature.

The mutation of seasons are keyed for him by animals associated with the changing weather of the year. On a June night he steps from his porch to watch a brilliant ballet of light done by thousands of fireflies dancing over a soybean field. They move in intricate patterns on a plane from two to four feet above the dark, green, prolific, teeming earth. W-Branch provides the orchestra for this ballet with singing frogs, crickets, cicadas, and a far-off whippoorwill. An occasional night hawk screams overhead. June is the season he associates with the mellow ring of the cowbell, sounding over the green land making a summer music and a dream that stays with him always. The fall of the year brings the high bark of a fox, the joyous tongue of the fox hounds, the mysterious call of the hoot owl. Winter comes and kills off the needling voice of the last insects. Then come the spring rains and it begins again.

Stuart often thought during this year of his recuperation of his strange mixed-up relations with Greenup, his home town. So much of his past life was tied in with a continuing battle with Greenup. Back in 1934 his first book, *Man with a bull-tongue Plow,* set off a spate of virulent criticism which lasted for twenty-five years. His school reforms antagonized half the town and led to his being brutally slugged on a side street in Greenup. In 1946 his novel, *Foretaste of Glory,* provoked so much personal vilification that Stuart and his wife discussed the possibility of moving away. But he got his fighting clothes on and dug in. Soon a new group was coming on, all the young people he had taught. They were firmly on his side, and they made the difference. His fame as a writer was bringing many inquiries to the town and the mayor asked him to do a pamphlet on himself to be mailed out from the mayor's office. Gradually the whole town swung over to his side and on October 15, 1955, Greenup celebrated "Jesse Stuart Day" with a huge celebration, a parade, speeches by notables, and the unveiling of a stone marker with Stuart's head and name. Stuart, with his doctor's permission, made a short and grateful speech. His twenty-one year war with his community was over. How did he feel about his victory? Like Wellington after Waterloo and General Meade after Gettysburg, he said—victorious but battered. But it was a happy ending.

For Stuart is basically a life-affirmer, a man who enjoys to the full the life he has been given in the strong masculine hill country of eastern Kentucky. And he would gladly live it all again:

> I would like to start my life over—borrow this same dust from the earth, have my same parents back, be born in the same little one-room log shack. I would like to write my high school themes again, use the same old fountain pen, see the same wild flowers, hear the same wordless song of the leaping stream. I would like to have my sheep back on this hill, have the hill green as it was then, with the clouds dropping down occasionally to visit and hide the woolly sheep. I would like to sell my first poem and my first story again, and write my first novel (p. 207).

His sickness brings his mind again and again to the leisurely heritage his own generation has had. Born into a world that gave them time to think, a leisure to grow in mind as well as body, they inherited a world of nature, a world God made. They lived an individual, not a collective, life. The children drove the cows to the milk gap to be milked. They heard the drowsy tinkle of the cow bell in a far pasture. They heard the fox horn blow at night. They had no telephones. They had a code of sounds and communicated with neighbors by notes blown on the fox horn. They had fox hounds, and whole families went to high ridges at night and fried chicken over an open fire and ate while listening to the chase. The stars were close, the air winy; and there was a poetry in those nights that Stuart can never forget. It is a heritage that he would never change for that of the present day.

One of the major motifs in the journal is death. Conscious as he is of how close he has come to dying, Stuart's mind broods over all his other escapes with death. They were numerous and more and more he feels that he is a fated man. He stops on one occasion just to enumerate them. Twice as a child he lay near death with typhoid fever. In high school he started spitting up blood and later learned he had survived an attack of tuberculosis. At Fort Knox a hysterical soldier pointed his rifle at Stuart at point-blank range and pulled the trigger. The bullet misfired. Stuart grabbed the rifle, ejected the cartridge, checked it, put it back in, pulled the trigger, and hit the bulls-eye. In the Ashland Steel Mills, Stuart worked the air hammer for six months. One night he was taken off and his substitute was killed by the malfunction of the hammer. Once in a fight he hit a man and knocked him out right before the man pulled a .38 on him. In 1938 Stuart received three severe blows on the head from a blackjack; the attending physician said they would have killed an ordinary man.

Once, in Mexico, Stuart was in a car that blew a tire at high speed, left the road, and rolled over seven and a half times. The other three occupants were severely injured; Stuart received only minor injuries. During the war years Stuart started to leave Washington on a six o'clock evening train. A vague premonition made him wait until the nine o'clock train, luckily, because the earlier train hit a rockslide and a large number of passengers were killed. In 1953 he escaped by one second more than a thousand tons of rock which struck the road where his car had been a moment earlier. Then in 1954 came the massive coronary. Truly he was a fated man. Stuart walked through the blur of the April woods and put his hand on the rough and smooth bark of the trees he had known since 1915: "When I am among them I laugh a lot. I never think about what is going to happen to me next. This would be getting ahead of schedule. I touch them and tell them I am a lucky man. I tell them I am one in a thousand" (p. 83).

Yet there is a more sober side to his reflection. One day in June he tries to carry some tobacco stalks up a gentle slope and develops an ache over his heart. He recognizes the warning and sits down to rest. As he rests there, he realizes that he is over the half-way mark physically and that he is watching himself slowly going out of the world: "In a way this is true of everybody. As we live, we die. We grow into the world and we grow out again. We watch ourselves slowly die" (p. 135).

Aside from Stuart himself, the man who dominates *The Year of My Rebirth* is Stuart's father. In February, Stuart paces about his house and yard looking continually up and down the road for a man to pass who never passes. He looks all day for this small wiry man who has made more tracks in W-Hollow than any other man. All through the cycle of the spinning year, the image of his father recurs. Although he is dead and buried in Plum Grove Churchyard, Stuart feels that he is ever near. How could he leave this place he loved so well?

In July, looking at the trees covering his seven hundred and fifty-eight acres of land and thinking how his own passion for conserving and improving the land was instilled in him by his father, he remembers how his father taught him that they must save land for generations to come. "And this is what I have done. I have lived in this valley all my life, and I own these acres in my heart. Man can never own them as securely by deed, for the land belongs to the people who love it and to the future generations of Americans" (p. 165). Wherever he moves up and down his valley, he encounters the invisible presence of his father, whose example has shaped and guided his entire life. Thinking of his father's death Stuart says, "I still find it hard to believe he is gone. This is why I think I hear him when it is only the wind in the willow leaves. I think I hear his hoe turning the stones over and over again in his corn row. How can he leave this world where his image is stamped so indelibly upon everything? He is still a part of this valley, just as it is still a part of him" (p. 99).

It becomes plain as *The Year of My Rebirth* unfolds that Stuart was the product of a remarkably close-knit family and that his father worked hard to knit and preserve these family ties. During the entire span of this year of his recuperation, Stuart's mind returns again and again to the warm family life of his childhood. These meditations appear throughout the year and are brought to a head, as December comes, by a long entry on the "suppertime" of his childhood. He remembers running home from school to do the chores in the brisk winter air. The supper bell rang and the hungry children rushed in to the table bountiful with farm food—with spareribs, sauerkraut, backbone, sausage, beans, onions, and hot biscuits. Cold milk and pitchers of buttermilk slaked their thirst.

Suppertime usually lasted three hours because everyone sat around and talked after eating. The parents, good listeners and good talkers, would tell tales of their childhood then listen to school experiences of the children. The father had a little game; he would take a different farm each night and tell how he would improve the place if he were able to buy it. He would tell where he would make meadows, have pastures, build a house, and set an orchard. When he got through talking, the children felt they owned these now beautiful farms. They left the table full of food and great dreams. The evening meal strengthened the family and welded its members into a unit that could not be broken. The father believed in a strong family unit; he taught them to stay together and to help one another.

With the end of December, this journal comes to an end. It has been not only a book of recovery, of recuperation, of walking up and down the earth again, but a book of return to the life and verities of his childhood. It is a book in which the author shifts his entire way of living. Once his world had been the skyways of America and the long trains that trailed across the continent: "Now my world was reduced to my home, my farm, my hills. I lived more closely with my wife, my daughter, my animal friends. I thought more deeply of my God. . . . This [1955] is the year of my rebirth, from my death to my morning" (p. 342). And the reader who has followed the month-by-month progress of the author through the long coiling spiral of the year feels the deep and lasting sincerity of this psychic rebirth. It is a book of the earth.

IV God's Oddling

In December, 1954, Stuart's father died. Jesse was weak and bed-fast, recuperating from his near fatal heart attack. Throughout the year of his recuperation the memory of his father haunted him. He kept looking for him on the roads and hills of W-Hollow, he kept listening for his step, he kept waiting for his knock. Out of this intense longing and anticipation came the realization that his father was the most extraordinary man that he had ever known and the person who had influenced him the most. He was a great man.

Looking back over his own work, Stuart realized that in a sense all through his writing life he had been writing the story of Mitch Stuart. The wiry, spirited little man ran through his poems, his stories, his articles; he was central to all. So out of his former writings, plus connective material written by Jesse especially for this volume, came the story of Mitch Stuart, *God's Oddling*. The title reflects the name Mitch Stuart had often used for his son, Jesse. He often called Jesse an "oddling" because he had an education, became a writer, and refused to smoke tobacco or drink the mountain moonshine. But, as his father approached death, Jesse began to think that it was really his father, the proud, independent individual, who was the "oddling"—"God's Oddling." Jesse feels strongly about this book: "This is the one book I have wanted most to write all my life."[9]

The book is really a kind of "Life with Father" suffused with humor and touched with the somberness of the hard life of the hills. Stuart's task was to choose from the best of the articles and stories about his father a series which could be arranged in a rough chronological order to give a sense of his life. He does this by picking stories such as "Nest Egg" and "Uncle Jeff" and writing headnotes and postludes to them. His interpolated comment provides a connective narrative which gives an impressionistic but gripping picture of Mitch Stuart from his wedding until his death—a unique, memorable picture.

As Jesse relates it, his parents' marriage had some rocky moments at the beginning. "They disagreed on just about everything—politics, religion and each other's friends" (p. 225). Pa was an iron-bound Republican and a Methodist whose father had served in the Union Army. Mom was a believing Democrat and Baptist whose father and uncles had fought in the Confederate Army. Because neither was shy about expressing personal opinions, there was plenty of friction and sometimes it got very hot. There came a day for instance, when Mom dressed her three children and got ready to go to her father's home. She was prepared to leave Mitch forever:

. . . . "I'm not coming back. I do not want ever to see this shack again. . . . Mitch, it's you. You can be laughing one minute and the next minute you can be raising the roof with your vile oaths. Your mind is more changeable than the weather. . . ." "We just aren't the same people," Pa says. "That's why I love you, Sal. You're not like I am. You are as solid as a mountain. I need you, Sal, I need you more than anyone I know in this world." (p. 11)

Mom is ready to leave when a spring thunderstorm comes up with a torrential roar of rain. As Mom walks about the house waiting for the rain to stop, she sees the wooden Martin boxes her husband made for her. As she paces back and forth, she sees other things—the split-bottomed chairs repaired by Pa, the clothesline, the nasturtium seed-box, the little wooden bench— all made by Pa for her. The rain ceases, the sun comes out, Pa looks worried. " 'The third time,' says Mom, 'that I've got ready to go. Something has happened every time. I'm not going' " (p. 18). The storm has blown over; and, arm in arm, husband and wife walk to the garden to see if the sweet potatoes have sprouted.

Pa grew to love his wife more and more as their marriage lengthened, but he never lost his fiery independence. There were other times when he felt put upon. One of these was when his wife's brother, Jeff Hilton, an enormous man, took to drink; he was more trouble, said Jesse, "than a cold collared mule in February." There was no one to take care of Jeff so his sister took him into her home. Pa's reaction was that "I'd rather have a copperhead in my house as to have your Uncle Jeff" (p. 98). But Jeff did the work of four men in the fields while he lectured Pa on the evil effects of alcohol on a man's body. He talked so convincingly that he had Pa afraid to take a glass of beer, but Jeff still managed to get to town on the weekends and to kill two gallons of moonshine.

A year passed, and Pa told his wife that Jeff must go because he was trying to run the farm. When Mom refused, Pa left. After six months word came to him on the Big Sandy that Jeff had "high-tailed it down the road," and Pa came back laughing; but when his wife tried to kiss him, Pa was leery. They argued and fought many a time but always came back together. He lived for three years after his wife's death; and, when death finally came for him, he lay on his bed and spoke about her:

> I've been lonesome without Sal for nearly three years and I'd like to see her. I don't mind sleeping in Plum Grove clay beside the only woman I ever loved. We had our ups and downs, Glennis. She was a Baptist and a Democrat and I was a Republican and a Methodist. Her Pap fit for the Gray and my Pap fit for the Blue and our house was divided but I loved her. All I have to do to see her again is just give up. Death's been following me for years but I wouldn't give up to him. You can tell Old Oddling I've changed my mind about the garden. Tell him I'm going on a long journey to see Sal and my people and my old friends. (p. 250)

And that was pretty much how it was between Mitch and his wife. Mitch had to be a strong, independent man because his life was hard. He left the Big Sandy country because of a feud. He came to Greenup County and started his married life in a one-room shack. He mined a coal bank, crawling back in it and working the coal on his back or belly. The hills were barren, and a farmer could not make a living on the land alone. Mitch moved into W-Hollow, cleaning up the land and putting in crops. When his little boy, Herbert, died of pneumonia, Mitch sat under a leafless apple tree in January, wrung his hands, and said: "It is too unbearable to stand. If we could have only had a doctor here in time to have saved him" (p. 19). A few years later, Pa rejoiced with a little baby boy, Lee; but the cold weather, primitive life, and pneumonia killed Lee in April, 1918. Only the very vigorous could endure this life.

Some prosperity came when Pa got work on the railroad as a section hand. There was plenty of food, and the children were being sent to school; but there were still reminders of the grimness of life in the hills. Pa was summoned to the funeral of his eighty-seven year old father who had been bludgeoned to death by feudists. The old man was buried at midnight on a hilltop in order to protect the mourners from attack. An aged soldier spoke a two-sentence eulogy, all that was said for Grandpa. Pa and his relatives walked quietly away in the night, leaving his father buried on a mountain high enough to overlook the rugged land of his people and his enemies.

Time and hard work eventually broke Pa's body. In his last years he suffered from a bad heart, rupture, high blood pressure, tumor, chronic indigestion, and underweight. For twenty-three years he had walked five miles to work on a railroad section and five miles back. In the winter he left by starlight and returned by it. On Saturdays he carried a coffee-sack full of groceries five miles from Greenup to his home. He worked on his farm constantly during all off hours. When he was a young man, a doctor had told him to put his affairs in order and prepare to die because he had a bad heart. But he had laughed at the doctor, and he continued to work hard until he was seventy-five. Only then did he give up and die. Life was hard, but he didn't complain.

Yet, in spite of the harshness of his environment, Pa lived a happy life. One of the greatest sources of pleasure for him was his land. He loved to pick up a handful of freshly plowed earth and fondle and sniff it. He hated to be rootless. He wanted to be firmly attached to his own spot of earth. The day finally came when he bought his own domain—fifty acres of wooded land that had no wagon road out. Pa came home that afternoon walking proudly. He was smoking a cigar instead of chewing home-grown Burley tobacco. He was a land owner. He cleared the land and preserved the soil. He sowed the first lespedeza seed seen in his section of the country. He cared for the soil with a passion, he was an earth poet who loved the land and everything on it. He would stop and stare with joy at new-ground corn sweeping up a steep hill toward the sky. He loved the smell of rich, green Burley tobacco maturing in the hot July sun. He pointed out to his little boy the beauty of raindrops on a redbird in her dark vest. He would talk with joy about the beauty of a rooster redbird, pheasant, chicken hawk, hoot owl, and turkey gobbler. He could sit for hours in the woods looking at a clump of violets growing beside a rotten log. He always kept a horse with a flaxen mane and tail because he liked to see one run in the moonlight with his mane high and his tail floating on the wind.

At the age of seventy, Pa cleared three-fourths of an acre in the heart of a wilderness right on a mountain top. He put a garden in and rejoiced in the delicious vegetables that grew in the virgin soil. The doctor had told him not to work at all, but he had to come back to this rich land. He explained to Jesse that after seventy, one was living on borrowed time and should go back to the places he knew and loved. He pointed down to the mountain slope below: "Your mother and I, when she was nineteen and I was twenty-two, cleared this mountain slope together. We raised corn, beans and pumpkins here. . . . That's why I came back up here. I went back to our youth. And this was the only land left like that was" (p. 220).

As Jesse matured and came more and more to understand his father, he realized how fundamentally his father was an earth-poet: "For my father had a world of his own, larger and richer than the vast earth that world travellers know. He found more beauty in his acres and square miles than poets who have written a half dozen books. Only my father couldn't write down the words to express his thoughts. He had no common symbols by which to share his wealth. He was a poet who lived his life upon this earth and never left a line of poetry—except to those of us who lived with him" (pp. 40-41).

Another source of Pa's happiness was his strong sense of family. After he had bought his fifty acres of land, Jesse and Jesse's Grandfather Hilton built a house; and the family moved in to stay for the rest of Mitch Stuart's lifetime. With his own land, with his own house and barn, and with money earned by his job on the railroad, Pa felt "well fixed"; and he rejoiced as the head of a big family. During the last year of his life he had the bodies of his two dead children removed from the remote hillside where they had first been buried, and had them reburied in Plum Grove near his dead wife. Buried there in the same plot, he affirmed in death the same family solidarity that he had affirmed in life.

No picture of Mitch Stuart would be complete that did not show his love of animals. He had a natural affinity for animals, and they all seemed to take to him. As a young man, he fed the mine rats and protected them because they had saved his life by warning him of an approaching cave-in. He had a succession of fine dogs—old Black-Boy, Jerry-B Boneyard, and Trusty Red Rusty. Two of them were fine snake-dogs, good at killing copperheads. Inordinately proud of Nest-Egg, his fine fighting cock, he turned down an offer of one hundred dollars for him only to have him killed by a tiny screech owl. Jesse cried over this incident, and his father had to wipe a few tears from his own eyes.

He had a soft spot in his heart for dove and quail, and he would not allow anyone to shoot them on his land.

But Pa got attached to his mule team of Dick and Dinah more than to any other animals he ever had. For seventeen years he had fed, cared for, and worked Dick and Dinah. The day Dick died was a dark one for Pa. He insisted on digging a grave at Dick's favorite resting place in the pasture and burying him there. By the time they got him buried, the rain was coming down, and Pa was wiping both raindrops and tears from his face. Pa never lost his love for animals, and just a few days before his death he instructed Jesse: "If anything ever happens to me and you live on, I want you to see to it that my horses stay right on this place till they die. I want you to see that old Lollipop stays here too, for your Ma thought so much of her. She's the last cow your Ma owned" (p. 242).

There can be no doubt that Pa comes alive for the reader as a many-sided, intriguing person. One of the main points of rapport is his speech. His talk is straightforward, highly idiomatic, and full of personality. As we listen to him speak, he comes sharply before us. For instance, Pa had never heard of Robert Frost, but he believed that good fences make good neighbors:

I tell you Sal, they don't make a better neighbor than old Fonse. Of course he don't belong to my party or my church. I can't help that, he can't help it. He's just what he is and I'm just what I am. But he's a good neighbor as a body ever lived by. It's good fences that we got between our places that make us good neighbors. You remember we couldn't get along with that hirm-skirm piece of a man that used to live over there. I built my part of a line fence and couldn't get him to build his. He would just brush it—keep throwing more brush on it. Cattle is smart these days on them brush fences after they've been used to barb wire. So his cattle kept getting in and eating up devilish nigh everything I had planted in the ground. Since Fonse has moved over there and bought that place we don't have any more trouble. (p. 73)

Pa describes how his wife started smoking: "—she has smoked ever since she was a little tot—smoked ever since she used to light her grandma's pipe and she drawled the stem to see if it was lit and she got a taste o' the smoke and you know how it is" (p. 159). He commends the work they've done in the corn field: "Yes . . . we've walked this work today" (p. 159). Whenever he talks, Pa speaks a pungent, fresh idiom.

By the time *God's Oddling* draws to a close, Pa has emerged as such a kinetic, dynamic individual, so wiry, tough, vital, and ongoing, so vigorous and earthy that it comes as a shock to us to see him falter, make a misstep, and almost fall as he leaves Jesse's front porch. Old death which has trailed Pa so long is finally catching up with him. A somberness falls over the book as we enter Pa's last days. Yet Pa dies as he lives, courageous, and pungent to the last. Doctors and family combined cannot keep him in bed until the day of his death. The pain finally becomes unbearable for him, and he gathers his family around him (except for Jesse, who is still bedfast from his heart attack). He has one small debt for cattle feed, and he instructs them to pay it. He is very conscious that, while he is withdrawing from the stream of life, the stream itself will flow on as vigorously as before. He points to his watch hanging on a nail above his bed: "Whitie, I've wound my watch for tonight. . . . In the morning I won't be here to wind my watch, so don't you forget to wind it and keep it running. Keep Doc, Bess and Lollipop, Whitie. And don't sell Tony [his prize bull]. You keep him" (p. 250). Then he gives detailed instructions about the caring for his wagon, manuring his garden, and liming his fields. He told his children that his feet had tickled the skin of W-Hollow earth more than the feet of any man living or dead, and that now he was ready to move on. Then he said: "Sophia, this is it. I am giving up. I am blind now. I am going" (p. 251). These were his last words. He began smiling, and he died with a smile on his face.

This memorable death befitted a man who was a "giant of the earth." When such a man withdrew from life he left, of course, a great absence about him. All through the following spring Jesse, who felt the absence of his father from the valley, thinks: "How can he leave this world where his image is stamped so indelibly upon everything? He is still a part of this valley, just as it is still a part of him" (p. 266). So the reader who puts down this book finds that the image of Mitch Stuart, God's Oddling, has been stamped indelibly on his imagination. We know we will look through many books and meet many a person in the world before we encounter the like of Mitch Stuart again. *God's Oddling* remains one of Stuart's great accomplishments—a tremendous encounter with a unique individual.

CHAPTER 2

The Poetry:
A Glory from the Earth

W HEN MORE than two thousand published poems lay behind him, as did the prestige of the Academy of American
Poets Award with its honor and its stipend, Stuart, then fifty-six,
wrote about the way he writes his poetry:

> When I write a poem or poems, I am moved by a mood which
> is often tied up with an incident. If I have the mood and don't
> have the incident, I will find one. If I have the incident and not
> the mood I don't write the poem or poems. I always write poems
> in long hand. I can't write them any other way. And I use black
> ink . . . sounds silly I know . . . [Stuart's ellipsis] but this is the
> way it is. The greatest number of poems I can remember writing
> at one sitting, forty-two, from fourteen to sixteen lines in a
> country churchyard on a Sunday morning. My mood had van-
> ished by noon. Poems are today in *Man with a bull-tongue Plow.*
> If I revised these poems, I had but little revision to do. I have
> written poems walking along the road, in walks among the trees,
> along the rivers, on trains, planes, buses . . . everywhere I have
> ever been. When the mood comes I almost have to write. Now,
> I usually let the poems lay over for days, maybe years, before I
> revise them. I let them "cool." Sometimes I revise a poem as many
> as ten times. I have to get one until it suits me. But I don't
> spend a lifetime on a few poems. They come to me. They have
> to be born. After they are born and in print I never want to read
> them again. I have no interest in them. Incidentally, I never use
> a plot or even a semi-plot (if such there be in a poem) but I
> merely use an incident.[1]

A short time before the above letter was written, Stuart had
published an article filled with a strong sense of foreboding. "A
few of the magazines still use my poems. Many which once used
them will not use them now. I find myself no longer on the in-

CARNEGIE LIBRARY
LIVINGSTONE COLLEGE
SALISBURY, N. C. 28144

side looking out, but I am now on the outside looking in. . . . Although my three volumes sold much better than the average books of verse I may never get another book published."[2] There is a strong sense of alienation from his poetic peers in these words. One is struck by Stuart's success as a poet of the people and by his later feeling of unease, a feeling in which he seems to search for some failing in his poetry which may prevent his attaining the highest quality. But Stuart may have found the flaw when he wrote that "Life on this earth at this time and place and among these people has been almost too full for me to do good writing. Living always comes first."[3] This dilemma is frequently discussed by critics, but great poetry can come from living life to the hilt. Perhaps Stuart gets closer to the crux of the problem when he writes—"Instead of my controlling poetry it has controlled me. I can only hope for quality since I have written quantity."[4] He is seized by his writing demon; for the most part he revises little since he would rather spend time writing a new poem than revising an old one. In brief, Stuart is a successful but somewhat unhappy poet.

For Stuart, turmoil, tension, and release are what poetry has always meant. Certainly Stuart was "born a poet"—if ever this could be said of a man. He has that organization of nerves and subconscious which demand outlet in a cadenced, verbal medium. When in his sophomore year in high school, Mrs. R. L. Hatton,[5] his teacher, introduced him to the poetry of Robert Burns, Stuart was ecstatic. He carried a volume of Burns around with him, stopping his work occasionally to read. When he was hunting at night he would read by lantern light while his dog coursed the uplands for game. He wore out several volumes handling them, and he longed to write poetry like Robert Burns's: "And my prayer, if ever I prayed one then, was to write poetry that would endure like the poetry of Robert Burns."[6]

I Harvest of Youth

All this youthful ecstasy produced an outpouring of verse, mostly imitative, and a book, Jesse's first—*Harvest of Youth*, published privately by Scroll Press at Howe, Oklahoma, in 1930; it drew little or no comment. Stuart was completely chagrined and, reacting against the book, refused to keep a single copy of it,[7] feeling it was a blemish. It is, of course, derivative; but it is what one would expect of a young poet just starting out and unable to break away from the phrasing of his current reading, and the poetry is certainly worth looking at for a moment in order to characterize the poet at the beginning of his career.

He dedicated the book (eighty-one poems in eighty pages) to his teacher at Lincoln Memorial Institute, Harry Harrison Kroll. It is arranged in four sections. Section One, "Out of the Night," probably took its title from W. E. Henley's "Invictus"; a mood of gloom and pessimism suffuses its constant preoccupation with death. Under "Epitaphs" in "My Landlord"—"But when he had to pass / Life's finished line, he did not leave / His shadow on the grass" (p. 20)—we hear the echo of *The Rubaiyat* in the last line. There seems also to be a definite admixture of A. E. Housman, as in "The Winner"—

> Against his will he ran a race with Death
> His muscles were taut drawn in every limb.
> His teammates saw him falter . . . lose his breath.
> They sought to cheer when Death romped by him. (p. 24)

Probably the best in this group is "Mountain Funeral" (pp. 22-23), based on an actual incident described in Stuart's *Beyond Dark Hills*. It begins sparely—"We could not stay about the house / Where so many were crying"— and then describes the stark look of the mountain home and fields newly deserted by the dead mountaineer. Its hushed specificity of country detail sounds a good deal like Whittier transplanted to the Appalachians.

Section Two, "Slabs From a Sun-Down World," reflects an obvious influence of Carl Sandburg and of the Imagists in its title and in its phrasing. The poem, "Undulated Season" (pp. 28-31), a loose free verse poem in the Sandburg manner, employs the lower case "i" *à la* e. e. cummings. "Steel Gang" gives us Sandburg's theme of the rough, unsentimental strength of the common man. "Silhouettes" (p. 32) is reminiscent of the general imagistic phrasing of Sandburg and of Ezra Pound's brief flirtation with the movement:

> Hard, clean
> Chiseled profiles
> Of black-bodied trees
> Swerving in the wind
> At sundown

Cold etchings . . .

Winter surface washed hills
Rain cutting a chalk gray
Skyline . . .

And last a leaning
Lean-to shack
Pressing in the dark

Only these
Silhouettes.

Stuart summarizes very aptly his Imagist phase: "In early days I imitated the Imagists—Glad I got in on the tail end of this miscarriage of poetry. But I decided to be what I am—no joining. No schools. The poet above all should be the individual and should communicate."[8]

Section Three, "Sonnets: Juvenilia," presents a rather curious mixture of styles ranging from "To Calloye,"[9] reminiscent of Edna St. Vincent Millay, one of Stuart's early enthusiasms; to "Personae," doubtless a title taken from Ezra Pound, the only non-sonnet in this section; to a series of rough, unorthodox sonnets which are of interest because five[10] of them were later incorporated into his *Man with a bull-tongue Plow.* In fact, with these unconventional sonnets Stuart seems to have stumbled on the idiom and medium which later made him a successful, widely read poet. They are mostly fourteen-line sonnets with no division of thought between octave and sextet. His favorite ryhme scheme in them is *abba, cddc, effe,* with a closing couplet, *gg.* Here Stuart was using a very flexible form which maintained just enough restrictions to preserve the general lineaments of the traditional sonnet. One of those sonnets, "To Muddy Waters," later printed as Sonnet 223 in *Man with a bull-tongue Plow,* had been submitted to an English instructor at Lincoln Memorial Institute. She had read it with displeasure and had advised, "Jesse, get away from these ugly things and write of high beautiful things like Shakespeare, Browning, Keats and Longfellow."[11]

The last part of the book, Section Four, "Harvest of Youth," is a kind of miscellany of thirty-two poems showing diverse influences—among them Burns in "Weather" and in "My First True Love" and Millay in "Empty Lover." This section is the poorest of the four and probably contains the earliest of the poems chronologically. The type of thing that later caused Stuart to squirm with embarrassment occurred in such sentimental, lugubrious poems as "She Ventured Far From God" and "Tennessee Farmer." This last poem is filled with bathos:

> Ott Davis spent his life on his farm
> In Tennessee he died.
> His children, Mary, Rube and Glennis
> Rotate wheat, rye and cane.

Stuart did not want to perpetuate this work. It is juvenilia of the type so often seen when a young poet is still self-conscious, still imitative, still a little afraid of launching out on his own. Yet he was a little too critical, because in it we do meet for the first time the rough, natural rhythms which become for him *the mode* in which his most successful work is written.

II Man with a bull-tongue Plow

Man with a bull-tongue Plow, published in 1934, really marks the apex of Stuart's poetic achievement. Between his high school years and the publication of this book came several key events leading up to this work that is described by the Irish poet A. E. (George Russell) as the greatest poetic work to come out of America since *Leaves of Grass*. For one thing, there was Stuart's stay at Lincoln Memorial Institute, where in three years' time he wrote about five hundred poems, received the encouragement of his teacher, Harry Harrison Kroll, and earned his bachelor's degree. He then passed to Vanderbilt where he studied for a year surrounded by the leading members of the Fugitive Movement, and came under the direct influence of that remarkable teacher, critic, and poet, Donald Davidson. Davidson, who recognized the true earthy nature of Stuart's genius, admonished him to stay away from the "arty" poems and to write about the farms and hillmen that he loved and about the constables and sheriffs whom he hated. Davidson read Stuart's poems, suggested revisions, and proffered names of editors and magazines for the young poet to mail his poems to.

Leaving Vanderbilt, Stuart returned to the hills of W-Hollow and said to his brother James: "I am going to write poetry to suit myself from now on. I'm in a different University . . . I'm going to be myself and write to suit myself and the way I damn well please. I've failed all my life. I can't do any worse than I have done."[12]

The apocalyptic moment struck him a short time later as he was plowing corn at the foot of the hill just opposite his house: he would write a book for his *own amusement* about the hills and the hill people. As the mules hooved up the dry, dusty dirt, Jesse wrote the first sonnet in a series which totaled seven hundred and three a year later. During that same dry, dusty summer H. L. Mencken published the slam-bang rhythm of "Elegy for Mitch Stuart" in *American Mercury,* and Stuart was launched for the first time in a name magazine.

Meanwhile, Donald Davidson was working to bring Stuart to the attention of a wider poetic public. He first had Stuart send some of his poems to Louis Untermeyer, who praised them. Then Davidson wrote a forceful letter of commendation to his friend Stringfellow Barr, then the editor of the *Virginia Quarterly Review*:

> My mountain friend, Jesse Stuart, writes me that he has submitted to you a MS of his sonnets. I hope very much that you'll give them serious consideration. If you are looking for an American Robert Burns, Stuart is the man—the first real poet (aside from ballad makers) ever to come out of the southern mountains. I know him well and have seen a lot of his work. But, even though I expected him to go along quite rapidly, I was astonished at what he had achieved in the sonnet series he sent me. He has an energy, intensity and a flow that simply staggers me. I hope, if you can accept some of his work, that you'll be moved to give him a good display,—one or two sonnets hardly show him to advantage. At any rate, I'll be personally grateful for any interest you may feel you can take. . . .
>
> There is nothing designing or pushing about him. I like him because he can write and yet not be "literary," in the silly modern sense. I still can't figure out how he managed to get an education and remain himself, quite unspoiled—but it happened.[13]

This effort brought about the publication of a group of twelve sonnets by Stuart in the October, 1933, issue of *Virginia Quarterly Review* under the title "Man with a Cutter Plow." A few days later the *American Mercury* published thirteen of the Stuart sonnets under the general title "Songs of a Mountain Plowman." In May, 1934, *Poetry: A Magazine of Verse* published still a third group of sonnets under the title "Young Kentucky." At about this time, when Stuart received an inquiry from E. P. Dutton and Company asking for more poems like the published ones, he went immediately to his dresser drawer, took out a huge batch of sonnets wrapped in a bath towel, and dispatched all seven hundred and three of them to the publisher. Very quickly the company returned a contract and a letter saying, "This is a great book of poems. It is like a big river with tributaries of life entering in. It is like a symphony of wind."[14]

Stuart's first copy of this book came to him early in August, 1934, at his farm home in W-Hollow. His mother, he said, took it in her hand and fondled it like a baby. His father shook his head in amazement: "I never thought you had a book in your head. I want you to read that book to me some time when we are not so busy with the work." [15] In October, 1934, when it was released to the public, a vast torrent of critical comment flowed over Stuart. All shades of opinion were expressed, most of it favorable. This book, which made Stuart a public figure, is in many ways a key to his thinking and to his life as an artist.

According to Stuart's own account, the seven hundred and three sonnets making up the *Man with a bull-tongue Plow* were written in a year's time. The general effect of the work is to give the ebb and flow of his life through the various seasons of the year, his memories of old times and former loves, and dramatic vignettes of comic or pathetic characters of W-Hollow and Plum Grove. Actually, the volume is a sort of commonplace book kept by a farmer who is also a poet. Subtitles divide the work into four sections, but we can move individual sonnets about and fit them into any one of the four sections with about equal justification. Stuart is equally loose with the sonnet form; his sonnets vary from twelve to seventeen lines in length. The scansion is frequently very rough;[16] the rhyme scheme is most frequently Shakespearean, but with many variations including occasional unrhymed lines. The poems may begin with strong lines and trail off to a weak, broken-backed conclusion; in other words, they give evidence of the haste in which they were composed. But, in compensation, they move with a kind of reckless, burning energy that sweeps the reader along through certain segments of the book. There is a kind of helter-skelter John Skelton air about these sonnets which adds to their charm.

If Stuart wrote Emblem poetry in the manner of Francis

Quarles (Quarles's popularity in the seventeenth century was as great as Stuart's in the twentieth), he undoubtedly would prefix *Man with a bull-tongue Plow* with a woodcut of a death's head, skeleton, or some other medieval symbol of death, because death is the central and focal topic of this book of sonnets. Something in Stuart's personal experience—his two brothers buried young on lonely mountain eminences, his paternal grandfather shot down by an enemy feudist, the frequent mountain-born babies who died in the first few days of their life, often preceded in death by their mothers—engrained far more deeply in him than in the average person the constant awareness that death conquers all. Consequently, he returns over and over to this theme throughout the sonnets, and—as we would expect of a young poet who had been reading voraciously before he began to compose—he echoes other poets. Sonnet 387, for instance, concludes with an obvious echo of Housman's *A Shropshire Lad*:

> Little their deaths matter to anyone
> And long for them the bull-tongue plows will wait;
> Their widows will go on and lie with men;
> Brothers to husbands, maybe—next of kin. (p. 198)

Housman also resounds through the conclusion of Sonnet 390, when Stuart ends a love poem with the stoic naturalism and phrasing peculiar to the English poet:

> There is a night I'd sleep beside of you
> And you would not know whom you slept beside;
> And we would sleep together the night through,
> This bridegroom never turning to his bride. (p. 199)

And E. A. Robinson's "Richard Cory" seems to be the unconscious source of Stuart's concluding couplet to Sonnet 473: "One Saturday he painted the town red, / Went home and put a bullet through his head" (p. 44).

Yet the most pervasive influence would seem to be Edgar Lee Masters. When many of the early reviewers noted the parallels between *The Spoon River Anthology* and *Man with a bull-tongue Plow*, they immediately concluded that Masters was a major influence. Stuart, however, denies that any conscious influence came to him from Masters: "I actually got the idea for the death section of *Man with a bull-tongue Plow* from Plum Grove Ceme-

tery. There is a stone there that gave me the idea."[17] Perhaps
a woodcut of Plum Grove Cemetery would be the proper *emblem* for this book.

Although death recurs throughout the four major sections as
a motif, it appears in varying modes. Sometimes it is the "Ubi
Sunt" motif of Sonnet 23— "Where are the friends of youth I
miss—Elmer and Bert, Oscar and Jim and John" (p. 14). At
others, the earth is welcoming the clay of a young man unjustly
shot down by the Law, as in Sonnet 113—

> And now, my friend, these hills would love to say;
> Comrade we drink your blood—your glorious clay
> We take into our arms at last to rest.
> We take you back, our son—gray-place in death.
> You gave unto the wind your fleeting breath. (p. 59)

Again it may be a stoic, somber description of a mountain
father burying his still-born child on a lonely hill:

> He took the bundle—hid it in the clay.
> He stood in silence then—I think he prayed.
> The crows swarmed over with their caw-caw calls.
> And Bill picked up the mattock—went his way.
> The lean hound slipped back to the grave and stayed. (p. 201)

Or Stuart is saying an affectionate farewell to his dead dog—
"Nig took the wrong trail when he took the track / Of Death—
We called but he could not turn back" (p. 203). Or Stuart's
macabre rejoicing at the death of a constable (so much like Sut
Lovingood's sadistic dislike of sheriffs) shot down while spying
on a moonshine still—

> The men next day saw old Bill stiff and cold.
> They said his mouth would make a trap for flies.
> One laughed and laughed and said: "God-damn his soul—
> He's snooping for the Devil—telling lies—
> We want the hungry hounds to bury him.
> We want piss-ants to come and eat their share.
> For what to hell's a low-down constable? (p. 215)

Or the poem may be a series of meditations on wives, lovers,
suicides, murderers now buried in Plum Grove Cemetery. Crimes
of passion are sprinkled throughout these sonnets. Mates caught

in flagrante delicto are invariably shot or knifed, and occasionally their unburied bones are left to bleach in the mountain weather, as is the case with Ol' Charlie Bull, who "harkened to 'Lid' Haily's lusty call" and was discovered by the husband Bill Haily, who gunned him down, and now "Pusley and careless hide white bones of his" (p. 262).

The meditations turn once or twice to the dead of World War I and to such native sons as Bill Tongs—"They brought him back from France wrapped in "Old Glory"— / Insolvent man for an old depository" (p. 275). The tone is always wryly deprecatory of that war and pretty much duplicates the anti-war sentiments of the writers of the 1920's and 1930's.

Frequently the sentiments about death are the commonplaces of nineteenth century Romanticism, but the cliché element may be relieved by a fresh effective image of death as in the "Clyde Jarvis" sonnet which concludes—

> But Death came by and complimented me
> Until I climbed into his two-horse surrey
> And Death and I drove his horses in a hurry.[18]

It is true, of course, that it is nearly impossible for a twentieth century writer to say anything new about death; indeed, Ecclesiastes gives the classic statement about death and no one has ever surpassed it. Stuart repeats the ancient modes and phrases, and the poems get some vigor from the mountain locale and mountain idiom. He achieves a certain freshness too in his dramatic sonnets which tell a little story in poetry and which are among his best. For example, one of the most memorable treatments of death in this volume occurs in a sequence of four sonnets about Rag Tussey,[19] who shot down his friend Tom Wilburn, and buried him in a series of shallow graves; digging his corpse up each night, he carried the stinking flesh to a new grave until he was caught one moonlight night and hanged. This haunting little drama is strikingly parallel to William Faulkner's famous story, "The Hound"; Stuart's clearly seems to have been published first.

So much preoccupation with death and man's all too evident mortality very naturally stirs the reader to wonder about resurrection. As he follows Clyde Jarvis, Dave Blake, Rag Tussey, and a hundred others to their cold mountain graves he wonders—will they rise? Will there be some rebirth for them? Stuart was never one to be coy with the reader, and throughout the long sonnet sequence he clearly implies a naturalistic end for all the men and women who go down into the earth: man dissolves back into the earth and becomes part of its endless supply of minerals and fluids. Stuart considers this theme important enough to be reserved for the last sonnet in the book, where a meditation on his own death concludes—

> "Now, I shall hold you down," said the warm clay.
> "I'll hold you down so you can never rise."
> Now if there is a Resurrection Day
> I shall be the one that's taken by surprise. (p. 361)

Yet if we stopped with Plum Grove Cemetery as the death emblem of *Man with a bull-tongue Plow*, we could not possibly explain the immediate hold the book exerted upon so many readers. The Freudian death-wish, so much bruited in the 1920's, still had not completely succumbed to the fashionable communism of the 1930's; but it was definitely declining in popularity. The appeal of the work was Stuart's love of life, his zest, vitality, and brashness. He begins by declaring unapologetically that he is "A one-horse farmer singing at the plow," and then he asserts in another sonnet his mountain man's long held conviction, "But we have got too goddamn many laws."[20] A vein of colloquial humor runs through this zest, emerging in the mock-romantic meditation on his love for the beautiful Annie Lee which concludes—

> But where is my sweet Annie Lee today?
> Ye faithful ties, I ask—oh, where is she?
> Somewhere she sits—a baby on her knee—
> I'm cockeyed sure it don't belong to me! (p. 36)

Or in Charlie Thombs's boast— "I heard Tom Murphey said I was afraid / Of him—W'y hell, I'd make Tom eat his dung" (p. 47).

This zest flows out into a kind of hilarious Vachel Lindsay myth-making in Stuart's sonnets on "Blind" Frailey, the fiddler who warms the feet of the country-ikes for their county-court day dance once a month. His imagination pursues "Blind" Frailey into heaven in a vision of the angels doing—

> The old Kentucky mountain "Waltz the Hall"—
> The most Kentuckyian of all dance calls—
> The Lord will sit in his high golden chair
> And watch "Blind" Frailey from Kentucky there,
> The Lord will sit wistfully a-looking on
> But the Lord will never say a word at all,
> Not when he sees his angels "Waltz the Hall—"
> And when he hears Frailey from Kentucky there
> He will sit back and laugh from his golden chair. (p. 69)

This gusto flows out too into Stuart's spring-song, an exuberant poem in which he praises the burgeoning vegetative glory of Kentucky and concludes in a very un-Shelleyan manner—

> Spring in Kentucky hills and I shall be
> A free soil-man to walk beneath the trees
> And listen to the wind among the leaves—
> And count the stars and do as I damn please. (p. 77)

It flows into his strong joy in the forms of earth and the pastoral joys of rest after country labor—

> I love to hear those red-oak night-winds sigh,
> Knowing that I shall soon be on my hearth
> And warm my feet before a good wood fire,
> Eat my supper—forget all worry—retire. (p. 115)

It speaks of his country independence, to which he adverts again and again—

> I sing for plowboys and the seedy sinners
> I pay my debts and do not bow to man.
> I live on the fruits of my sweaty labors—
> I hate the law—God damn the politician—
> I divide without a fuss among my neighbors
> I live among the earth a dirt-colored man.
> I'm just an ordinary citizen. (p. 174)

In *Man with a bull-tongue Plow* we also find laments for lost loves and romantic brooding over the transiency of youthful love. We anticipate this poetry because of the immense vitality of the poet, and a sizable number of the sonnets do depict the various women who caught the eye of the poetic speaker. Yet these sonnets are among the poorer of the sequence because they seem a little too derivative. Echoes of Robert Burns are many in these love sonnets as, "Jean Torris, you and I have gone together. . . . When winds were sobbing in the mountain heather" (p. 228). We cannot escape Burns as we read about Stuart's highland lasses. Some of these poems teeter on the edge of bathos and occasionally collapse into it as, "I shall not go inside the church tonight. She must not see me stagger down the aisle" (p. 84). Occasionally, he grows oppressively Poesque as in the repeated chiming of "Lydia Doore" in the five sonnets about this too euphonious lady.[21] The themes are the ancient ones of mutability and *carpe diem;* no new twists appear. The emotion seems too studied; the language is repetitious. The best thing about them is the occasional felicitous image drawn from the mountain milieu. Too self-conscious about his poetic loves, Stuart is happier with other subjects.

Such a subject would be the poetic vignettes or character sketches scattered throughout this book. Sonnets 465-474, for instance, tell stories of wives, lovers, murderers, and suicides—all asleep in death in Plum Grove Cemetery. The best of these poems have the quality of good brief narrative. Sonnets 475-486 tell the story of Anice Bealer, a profane "By-God" old man who farms, loves open air, gets a token of his death (a shaving paper blows out of his hand onto a grave), and laments the fact that his children will come back to dispute over his estate. He dies as the token predicted he would; he has dreamed of a heaven which is simply his own farm writ large ("For after death I'd love to plow again" [p. 246]); and he departs leaving nine children fighting over his land and his gold. This narrative vein seems to be the mode for which he is best suited in his poetry; indeed, Stuart's short story "Three Hundred Acres of Elbow Room"[22] grew out of these poems about old Anice Bealer.

Considerable space has been devoted to this book because, as already stated, it is a key work in the Stuart canon. When Stuart stopped his plow on a summer day and scribbled his "I am a farmer singing at the plow"[23] sonnet, he was marking a decisive moment in his writing career: he began to draw from his own pungent mountain material for his poetry and fiction and to release the resources of his preconscious and subconscious mind. Some casting up of accounts on *Man with a bull-tongue Plow* are helpful, therefore, as a perspective on the later works. On the debit side would be the salient fact that there are simply too many sonnets in the collection. This "too-manyness" is really the major defect of the book. Too many in the same tone lead to monotony; too many on the same subject, to boredom; too many unpolished ones weaken the total effect; and too many derivative ones detract from originality. From this date and this distance it seems clear that Stuart and his editor would have produced a greater work had they carefully culled about three hundred of the best sonnets, polished these carefully, and published a compact and succinct book. It is easy, however, to see why the editor was overwhelmed by this great river of poetry and why he wanted to keep the impression of opulence, freshness, and vitality by letting it flow over the reader.

And there is something to be said for this objective. The result as published is a work with mixed effects: a kind of "Rubaiyat of Jesse Stuart," plus a "Kentucky-Shropshire Lad," plus a "Plum Grove-Spoon River Anthology." The human feelings expressed hold the reader rather than the verbal artistry. The poems themselves do not have the close packed, dense meanings of so-called "modern" poetry. They present a great, vital picture of a community and of a personality in language which has the diffuseness and openness of certain sonnets of Shakespeare, such as the "Full many a glorious morning have I seen" sonnet, which has drawn open disdain from John Crowe Ransom and other practitioners of the modern metaphysical style. There are many contemporary readers, however, who like this open style when used by Shakespeare; and they like and will continue to like Stuart's version of it in *Man with a bull-tongue Plow*. This book is a moment in American poetry, but a lasting one.

III   Album of Destiny

In contrast to the slapdash speed (eleven months) with which Stuart produced *Man with a bull-tongue Plow*, he labored eleven years over *Album of Destiny* (1944), his second major volume of poetry. The idea for this work had come to him in 1932 as he idly turned through the pages of an old family album which showed pictures of his youthful mother and father, posing before apple trees in bloom. Later pictures showed them worn and aged, and Stuart thought how he who was now young and in the vigor of his life must complete the same cycle that his parents had gone through. Then the idea came to him of a volume in which he would show a group of people through the four seasons of their life. He first planned to do this with a hundred people, but soon cut the number to fifty. He planned four portraits to correspond to the four seasons of life, then a section in which the children of these people would speak and write, thus accomplishing a kind of physical resurrection of their parents' lives.

He immediately began to write poetry for this volume. Before he was through, he had written two thousand poems which had been set down in forty-one different states and many foreign countries (six were composed while Stuart was a house guest of Lady Astor at her London home). All were extensively revised (some as much as ten times); and, after systematic culling, four hundred and twenty-three were published. His intention was to show his little mountain community as a microcosm of the great world; and, by explaining it, to explain all. In this sense, of course, the volume is akin to Whitman's *Song of Myself* and to Masters' *Spoon River Anthology*.

In structure, the book consists of twelve different sections of poetry, each with a descriptive title. John and Kathaleen Sutton, the central characters, stand for Everyman. Each season is treated in two separate sections (spring, for instance is covered by "Sonatas of Spring" and "Our Rights to Spring"); and, as we move through these long seasonal divisions, we meet many diverse characters and find a poem devoted to each character in each of the sections. To follow any one of these characters through the four seasons is to follow the story of his or her life in brief. The most detailed of these stories is, of course, the story of John and Kathaleen. Section 10, "Songs of Destiny," gives us a short interlude of poems spoken by the twelve children who survive John and Kathaleen; Section II, "Their Resurrected Spring," permits the children of all the characters treated in the seasonal poems to speak their finales. Thus we have the great wheel of time turned through four seasons and on into the future through the children of the race with each person, as it were, forming for a while a spoke in this great wheel.

To frame this study of time and man, Stuart provides a "Prologue" and an "Epilogue" to show the beginning of earth-time and the swell of America into the generations of the future. He gets his effect by allowing the natural world to speak—the grass, wind, snakes, scorpion, and lizard—the world of earth which is so completely Jesse Stuart's own; but the saurians and reptiles are also symbols of evolutionary beginnings of life.[24] Life and death and the inevitability of suffering and death are his great themes. The immortality that he offers is that through the children who carry on the work of their sires. His intent seems clear—this book is intended to be a great tragic paean—a spacious panorama of Man's vexed journey toward death on this earth. It is a vast and elemental and age-old theme—echoes of Ecclesiastes, Virgil, and Shakespeare roll through it.

Its form again is the "Stuart Sonnet" (fourteen or sixteen lines, with varying rhyme schemes), but these sonnets are much more carefully worked out technically than those in his first volume of poetry. Most of the sonnets are identified by the name of the speaker (as "Tobias Bently" or "Lacey Caudill"). Where there are no names at all at the top of the sonnet, the poet is the speaker in his private lyric voice. The poet himself under his old fictional name of Shan Powderjay ends each long section with a poem, just as he does by closing the "Ascension of Autumn" section with a sonnet which contains these titular lines:—

> Through soft eyes of the grass I can discern
> Album of Destiny's fine photographs,
> Worn out by years of living, they return
> To wooing worms of earth and epitaphs.[25]

A few of the poems antedate *Man with a bull-tongue Plow,* but the majority were written after its publication. Stuart based his characters largely on people that he knew. He rushed the concluding sections into shape during 1943 (he regretted this hurry later) before he went to boot camp in the navy, and he read proof on it while he was completing the hectic routine of training.[26] Two fellow poets—Louise Townsend Nicholls and William Rose Benet—gave him helpful critical suggestions with the closing poems in the volume.

When *Album of Destiny* was given no favorable attention by critics, Stuart was chagrined. He had thought the plot would make this book a kind of novel in verse with colorful characters spilling from every page, or perhaps the analogy would be better stated as a kind of musical pageant of people's fleeting days on earth where their joys and trials were recorded in carefully chosen words. To this day Stuart has not reconciled himself to the critics' judgment. Yet we, going back over the volume and assessing it carefully, must agree that this work does not live up to Stuart's expectations and that it does not equal the appeal of *Man with a bull-tongue Plow.*

There seem to be at least two reasons for this failure. First, Stuart, in his attempt to make this his *best* poetic work, worked too hard at it, revised too closely, and became much too self-conscious about it. Stuart, like Thomas Wolfe, listened too closely to his critics, and in pacifying them, he lost some of the spontaneity which was his great charm in his earlier volume. Second, he has again included too many poems on the same theme. The resulting monotony and the failure to modulate into different keys of emotion detracts from the book when it is read as an organic unit. Stuart chose a great, lofty theme, and then tried to live up to it; we miss, therefore "the dirt-colored man, the ordinary citizen" who gave so much color to the *Man with a bull-tongue Plow.* If he had picked a less lofty theme and relaxed, he would have had a better book.

William Butler Yeats wrote that "all art should be a Centaur finding in the popular lore its back and strong legs." Stuart had the back and strong legs of the centaur in the sense that he had absorbed the popular lore of his region probably better than any writer in the United States (with the possible exceptions of William Faulkner and Elizabeth Madox Roberts). He adequately conveys this knowledge in his short stories, but he fails to do so in *Album of Destiny* in a great number of poems; and this failure seems to be the fundamental one of the book so far as diction is concerned. In his short stories his words are vascular and alive; as a result, some of his stories—such as "Thanksgiving Hunter"— have the force which much of the poetry of *Album of Destiny* lacks. Although Louise Cowan remarked that Jesse Stuart lacked the "pietas"[27] of Southern poetry, this statement seems manifestly untrue. Stuart does have the "pietas," but he lacks the grace of idiom to convey it justly. Why Stuart can use the idiom in the short story and not in the poem is difficult to answer—perhaps inexplicable, even to him.

IV   Kentucky Is My Land

In 1952, Stuart brought out *Kentucky Is My Land,*[28] a small volume arranged under seven different headings which contains poems showing his love for the diversity of his native state. Part

One, "Kentucky Is My Land," begins with the title poem—a long, discursive work in free verse paragraphs of varying lengths and in rather prosaic language—which praises Kentucky as the heart of the United States, showing how it differs from East, West, North, or South. "Kentucky Is My Land" was commissioned by a farmer magazine for an issue featuring the state. Stuart composed a prose piece first, but his wife pointed out that it read like poetry so he lined it off as free verse and it was so published. The general tone and style, reminiscent of Sandburg, never quite escape their prose origin. Stuart does catalogue the multifold appeal of Kentucky, but the portrayal fails to come alive and vibrate as it does in the living scenes of his best fiction.

Part Two, "The Ballad of Lonesome Waters," begins with a poem of that title which tells the story of a mountain love affair and shooting, written in a galloping, on-going meter, heavy with perfect rhymes, all being used to point up the old Kentucky proverb: "In lonesome waters when you drop a dime, / It may be long but you'll return sometime." The best line in the poem is "Nine hound-dogs meet them . . . Their front teeth pretty as a monument," which is fresh and good and the type of figure that appears more frequently in Stuart's stories than in his poetry. "The Cities" denounces the gray, money-mad cities in favor of the lonesome waters and beautiful earth of Kentucky. "Elegy For Mitch Stuart"—a lusty, roistering elegy (about as lively as an elegy can be)—has big, booming onomatopoeic effects suggesting Vachel Lindsay. One of Stuart's early poems and one of his best, it praises Stuart's grandfather, "Old Mitch," as a tough, hell-raising feudist who unceasingly fights the Van Horns and marches in the parades on his game leg right up to his dying day. His epitaph:

> Old Mitch's a-fightin still,
> He's got 'em on the run . . .
> One hand is on his bottle,
> The other on his gun. (p. 33)

In Part Three, "Songs For Naomi," we find a series of sonnets (some fourteen lines, some sixteen lines) celebrating the calm delights of married love. Images of love, domesticity, time, the woods, and farm intermingle. There is a continual praise of the lares and penates of the farm home which is frequently good but sometimes hovers close to the bathetic as in the lines:

> While coffee hot, with eggs our hens do lay,
> And wild grape jelly, bacon from our farm
> Make us a good beginning for the day. (p. 38)

Here Stuart is attempting the Horatian Sabine-farm note which has been done most successfully in English poetry by Robert Herrick in "His Grange, Or Private Wealth" and in "A Thanksgiving To God For His House." It is a deceptively simple note and not at all easy to achieve in a natural and seemingly guileless manner, yet Stuart does bring it off in a moderately successful way in these poems. The rhyme scheme is primarily Shakespearean, and the diction frequently echoes Shakespeare's sonnets as in the lines: "For you, my love, are fairest of the fair / And Time, your enemy, I most despise" (p. 38).

Part Four, "Poems For My Daughter," are among the best in this book. In clear, unforced, loving sonnets Stuart meditates on the beauty and mystery of his infant daughter as she sleeps. She lies in a cocoon of innocence, and the parents are bemused with wonder before this innocence, and they think with nameless emotions of that future experience which must bring her knowledge of pain and evil.

In Part Five, "Songs Of A Mountain Plowman," Stuart assembles some thirty odd sonnets (both fourteen and sixteen line sonnets) which treat a cross section of mountain themes. "May I Be Dead" is a low-keyed wish that the poet die before all of this natural beauty—ferns, trees, hills, and river—is altered by industrial change. The constant, gnawing beauty of the natural world is the most frequent theme in this section and culminates in the lyric "I Cannot Write Tonight" which pulls the poet from his study into the beautiful moonlit world of a mountain winter where he wanders and thinks a *Rubaiyat* thought:

> Remember hills stay young; their beauty keeps
> Eternally as seasons come and pass;
> They will be here when this admirer sleeps
> Who will not leave his shadow on their grass. (p. 71)

Two of the better poems speak of his parents: "Her Work Is Done" is a tender memoir to a mountain mother who in Stuart's youth was a forceful river of strength, strength which was spent in a lifetime of labor on the mountain slopes; her time has passed, and now the strength ebbs away. "Prayer For My Father" is a quiet petition that his father, whose life has been eaten away in hard manual labor, will have some leisure days without a care before death takes him gently by the arm.

Part Six, "Great Lakes Naval Training Station," contains the nostalgic sonnets of a hillman who looks back with love and regret to his family and mountain home before going overseas. This sequence climaxes with one of Stuart's better sonnets, which begins:

> Remember if this man is lost at sea
> In feathery fathoms of its midnight deep
> And waves can't break my brain's last secrecy
> These will be images that I will keep.

(The third line above is a good one and smacks a good deal of John Donne, an unusual occurrence in Stuart's work.) The poet then lists the images of morning hills, his mother at work, tobacco in the fields, the beauty of his wife's face, of his daughter at play in the living room. All these he willingly sacrifices for freedom's sake. This poem makes Stuart one of the few contemporary poets willing to write about wartime sacrifices without derision.

This relatively short volume ends with one long poem which makes up Part Seven, "The Builder And The Dream." This poem records the dream of a boy, Ben Tuttle, whose vision was to reforest the denuded hills of his childhood valley. As a man he buys, little by little, the wasted land; plants it with trees; and lives to see the thousand wasted acres changed to a beautifully forested mountain region which people come to and admire. The poem recounts a real accomplishment of Jesse Stuart, who actually did in W-Hollow what Ben Tuttle does in the poem: he brought back beauty to the people; he produced a great forest. The deed is admirable, but the language of the poem is a little high flown. Not a great or a good poem, it does describe a great and good act—an act potentially far more valuable than most poems. This is probably the best way to summarize the entire volume, *Kentucky Is My Land*—it is not great poetry, and it lacks the tumbling kinetic energy of *Man with a bull-tongue Plow;* but in it Stuart speaks of great and good acts with sincerity.

V Hold April

Between the publication of *Kentucky Is My Land* (1952) and *Hold April* (1962), Stuart suffered his nearly fatal heart attack. *Hold April* is evidence of the marked influence this attack had on his thinking in general and on his attitude toward religion in particular. All in all, this entire volume is more subdued in tone, more relaxed, more religious—a new note of acceptance of the burdens and vagaries of life has crept in. Divine intervention alone—as Stuart says repeatedly in *The Year Of My Rebirth*— was the sole cause of his survival. The love of country things remains strong, as does his distrust of cities, tranquilizers, and high-powered autos. In a poetic sense, Stuart sounds more like Robert Frost than like Robert Burns.

A glance at the table of contents of *Hold April* indicates that there is no attempt to impose a unifying framework on these poems, as there was in his first three voluumes of poetry. He has taken the best of the poems and put them together to show the nature of his poetic thinking in the last few years.[29] The central poem in the entire book is "Dawn,"[30] which is also the longest (seven pages); and it is virtually a microcosm of all the themes which appear in *Hold April*. In this emblematic poem, the speaker rises in the pre-dawn night, walks over the roads of the earth to a high hill, and watches the giant earth waken and come to life—"Each spur of ridgeline . . . a mighty finger" (p. 56). Throughout the poem, the autumn scene carries overtones of Stuart's autumn of life, one in which he has found joy, love, and peaceful acceptance. The giant earth speaks of hidden, immense things through the songs of a pair of wild birds "talking to each other in the night" (p. 59). The speaker knows that he is but dirt borrowed for a time from the giant earth on whose skin he walks. He plays a game of hide and seek which soon must end when, "The little that I have borrowed from him [earth], I shall return with interest" (p. 60). The transition of the earth from summer to autumn has been the transition in the speaker's heart from darkness to light, "From death unto the morning" (p. 61).

> After I spoke to Death and shook his hand
> He left me with my new lease on life.
> I vowed the second half should not be spent in vain.

> Wherein I witnessed a rebirth
> Where God's own light dissolved the darkness
> In conflict for the final power. (p. 62)

Thus this poem works from the ancient death and rebirth arche-
type and affirms Stuart's commitment to an ethically purposeful
life until his second and real death. The poem moves with echoes
of the Old Testament, Elinor Wylie, and even Thomas Wolfe;
and it achieves a genuine dignity.

In contrast to this serious and moving poem is his comic poem,
"Free Ride," describing the boorish manners of a free loader
(who happens to be a fly) on an airplane flight from Dallas to
Chicago. In clipped iambic trimeter stanzas, Stuart sketches a
vignette of the fly as "A pestering airways guest" who rushes to
the door as the plane lands:

> Ignoring signs and manners
> And those he rushed before.
>
> Soon as the door was opened
> And steps for us let down
> This Texas fly was greeting
> A fly whom he was meeting
> In big Chicago town. (p. 72)

This poem about a Texas fly who bears a marked likeness to the
big wheelers and dealers of current Texas fame is a skillful beast
fable, a modern version of Aesop that reminds many readers of
Robert Frost's "Departmental."

Stuart, deeply committed to family, commemorates the death
of his mother, that staunch and beautifully spirited woman who
lives in so many of his poems and stories, in "For Martha Hylton
Stuart," a finely restrained tribute of sixteen lines which has the
place of honor as the last poem in the book. "Soft, velvet grass
erases all the scar / Where she now lies embedded for the
night . . ." (p. 110). Embedded for eternity in Plum Grove clay,
this strong-willed mother returns after death in her son's revery,
and "Heart-Summoned" is the poet's description of this poignant
return:

> Sometimes in bonnet that she used to wear
> And faded dress by wild-rose brambles torn,
> She moves so lightly on her path of air
> As she returns, a mother to her son.

> She does not knock nor does she come within
> To tell me who her new companions are:
> She vanishes upon her path of wind,
> Accompanied, perhaps, by cloud or star.[31]

The heart attack which so wrenched Stuart's life and revitalized his thinking is noted in his brief poem "One body" (p. 99), which speaks of the furious drive which hurled this body "through its youth and prime" into more diverse things than one body can do, until "there came a time" and it collapsed into the long hiatus of a massive heart attack. This poem's description of the blind energy which whirled him into such prodigal expenditures of his vitality sounds remarkably like the famous apostrophes of Thomas Wolfe to the "Fury" which hurled Eugene Gant into constant, frenetic endeavors throughout *Of Time and the River*.

Again and again God stoops into these poems, showing how deeply the poet was affected by the closeness of death, as in the poem, "Back where I belong":

> Death held me prisoner till God stepped in
> And took me by the arm and gave me breath,
> And I was glad this heart was cleansed of sin
> And that I followed him from arms of death. (p. 86)

This note of acceptance of the inscrutable divine will—a note completely absent from the seven hundred-odd sonnets in *Man with a bull-tongue Plow*—shows again in "Why ever grieve," which justifies the deaths of autumn and of man with spring resurrection and man's new life:

> With wordless blueprints from eternity
> Nature will reproduce the broken parts,
> Make flowers grow from old roots in the sod
> When we can't grow new arms and make new hearts,
> Don't question man but ask Almighty God. (p. 21)

Thus Stuart affirms that God ultimately ordains the grievous pattern of the universe, and affirms his acceptance of the mystery of pain and suffering. This wisdom is summed up in a little poetic parable, "Once on a solitary walk," which could have dropped straight from Thoreau's *Walden*. The poet on his solitary walk through a wilderness discovers a small peach tree growing out of wasted land. He plucks the three beautiful peaches from the topmost branches and eats:

> The most delicious fruit I ever knew,
> The sweet lush flesh of red October cling,
> Such fruit from this small seedling tree that grew
> From earth so poor it scarce could grow a thing
>
> Where sassafras, sawbrier and sumac thrived,
> This fruit tree never had a guiding hand,
> Smothered in sterile soil, yet it survived,
> A good seed dropped upon a fruitless land. (p. 53)

This poem more or less confirms the general tone of *Hold April*: life is a cross-grained, difficult experience, with good and evil inextricably mixed; yet it is ultimately worth enduring, because the small good acts of life, though choked in bordering evil, yet survive like "A good seed dropped upon a fruitless land."

Hold April gives us nothing new in technique or genre, and it lacks the heedless energy which coursed through *Man with a bull-tongue Plow*. But it does show Stuart abandoning the pessimistic naturalism of his early poetry for a God-centered universe. This point of view is expressed so clearly that it seems safe to affirm it as Stuart's mature attitude at his present position in life. In this sense, the volume carries a kind of finality about it which makes it an important work in the canon of Stuart's writing.

CHAPTER 3

The Short Stories:
Tales of Shan and Others

WHEN the definitive history of the American short story is written, Jesse Stuart's name may well be near the top of the list of the best writers in this genre. For Stuart, in the time-less vignettes of his short stories, has done what every great writer longs to do. He has created a *place* and wedged it ever-lastingly in the imagination of America. His stories have given a voice to the far and lost land of the Appalachians, a voice which calls us ever and delightedly into the outdoor world. The reader of any volume of Stuart short stories opens the book and feels immediately the fine mist of nature blowing into his face. This is the world that Stuart has made in the medium of the short story, and it can no longer be ignored by serious critics.

It would be difficult, for instance, to ignore the three hundred and forty short stories by Stuart which have been published in magazines ranging from the slicks to the littlest of the little magazines, stories cutting across all the social strata of America in their appeal. Stuart, like Wolfe, contemplates the life he knows and puts it into words—he is more interested in the life than in the writing, if we understand by "writing" self-conscious absorption in technique. The broad appeal of Stuart's short stories derives primarily from the attraction of Stuart's fictional "world." Stuart heeds the hoariest of all writing axioms, "Write about what you know." Practically speaking, all of Stuart's short stories are projections of the eastern Kentucky milieu into a fictional world. When we open a volume of Stuart's short stories, any volume—*Plowshare in Heaven, Clearing in the Sky, Head O' W-Hollow*—we are immediately in the *ambiance* of W-Hollow. W-Hollow is a world of hills and mountains, dark hills in the wintertime but marvelous flowering hills in the spring. We move along bony ridges, or down mountain hillsides covered with "tough-butted white oaks" (an obsessive phrase with Stuart), or through fertile valley land. We pass through the dry, dusty, baking heat of July with sweat drops big as white soup beans forming empathically on our faces and marking our trail in the dust. Or we ride on a mule with Shan Powderjay through the bone-chilling blasts of a February night and dismount to knock the balls of clotted snow from the hooves of the mule. The land is hard, somewhat primitive, and its people make their living by hardscrabble farming, cattle-trading, mining, timbering, or moonshining.

Primarily of Scotch-Irish or of English stock, the people bear old-fashioned names: Big Eif Porter, Battle Keaton, Uglybird Skinner, Symanthia Fiddler, Jason Whiteapple, Cief Salyers, Zeke Hammertight, Grandpa Birdwell, Snort Pratt, Adger Wampler, Subrinea Boone, Sweet William Hawthorne, Tilden Dingus, Birdneck Sweetbird. The dwellers in W-Hollow are a simple, direct people with strong passions and, usually, long lives. They take their religion fairly seriously whether they are Methodists or Baptists, the only two religions that established a strong foothold there. The Baptists are particularly vigorous in spite of having fragmented into such picturesque groups as the Forty-Gallon Baptists, the Free-Will Baptists, the Slab Baptists, the Hard-Shell Baptists, and the Foot-Washing Baptists.

Family loyalty, as strong as religion, leads to some spectacular feuds; but the unwritten law is that one never shoots his own kin, whether kin by marriage or by blood. All of these families are superstitious to an extent, and they have a particularly strong belief in tokens. If Big Eif Porter receives a token that he will die at ten that night, he prepares for it and peacefully passes away right on the minute. Death comes often by violent means, frequently by guns and sometimes by the ubiquitous copperheads, rattlesnakes, and water moccasins who are always in wait for the unwary mountain man. Then comes a mountain funeral: the dead man is provided with a homemade coffin and buried with a four-hour-long sermon on some hilltop belonging to the family.

Although these people live a hard life, laboring long over the meager soil for scanty returns, they also have their relaxation. There is the sweet solace of tobacco, to be chewed by the men or smoked in short-stemmed pipes by the women. There is the burning pleasure of mountain moonshine, varying from that "ol' *mean* fighting kind of moonshine" to "the real yarbs," which is the very best. There are protracted meetings at Plum Grove Church, basket dinners with huge supplies of food and moonshine on the side, the courtships by the "young 'uns," and the sporadic and joyous fights of the young bucks. Fox hunting provides a long nighttime delight to the males of all ages. Guns are a major source of pleasure to the men who occasionally "spice up" dull times by lying on different sides of the Sandy River and firing away at each other for fun.

There are various other pastoral rites of pleasure, including frog-trouncing—a game in which a plank and a wooden mallet are used to hurl a frog high into the air—which seems to be peculiar to the environs of W-Hollow. Love is direct and uncomplicated, and marriages come early, usually marked by the "Bellin' of the Bride," which includes prolonged gunfire from as many shotguns as there are men present. But of all the joys into which the hard-working mountain people escape, none compare in their orgiastic abandon with the hangings. People—men, women, children, infants—pour in from the hills and valleys, excursion boats, to witness the great hangings, like the hanging of the Sixeymore brothers when the band played "Dixie" and the dying men cursed and blackguarded the gaping multitude. Women fainted, men fought, and six sheriffs packing big guns circulated through the crowd, trying to keep law and order.

Beyond all this furor lies the poetry of the earth, which is never dead for Shan Powderjay, the fictional alter ego of Jesse Stuart. Walking in the moon shadows on a June night, listening to the clear bell tones of a foxhound on a cool October night, gazing from a clearing in the sky to the mountain lowlands below—all of these are phases of the inexhaustible delights of nature ever present to the man who follows the bull-tongue plow along the hilly furrows of W-Hollow.

The world of W-Hollow is the fictional world of Jesse Stuart, and there can be no doubt of Stuart's attitude towards it. He likes it, and his feeling of pleasure in this almost-vanished world is communicated with unmistakable gusto. It is a strong three-dimensional world, possessing solidity, depth, and permanence. Like the Pigeon River country of Elizabeth Madox Roberts and the Yoknapatawpha County of William Faulkner, it is a good, interesting, and permanent addition to the literary geography of

America. But the pull of Stuart's short stories cannot be completely accounted for by the fascination of the world of W-Hollow. Much of his hold on the reader comes from his impelling method of narration, a rigorous propulsive force which, in his best stories, hastens the reader pell-mell to the conclusion. One of Stuart's earliest writing mentors, Professor Harry Kroll, told him to stick to poetry because he would never be able to write publishable short stories. But Stuart disagreed; and now more than three hundred published stories later, Professor Kroll has acknowledged his error.

To become a writer of short stories Stuart wrote and destroyed stories until he developed his own technique and saw his first story, "Battle Keaton Dies," published in *Story* magazine. Given Stuart's method of narration, almost anything he writes takes on a gripping interest, and the essence of his tale-telling is its oral character. Stuart uses the famous "talk style" that came into American fiction from the folk tale, the humorous tales of the old Southwest, and the countless raconteurs of nineteenth-century rural America, culminating in the often masterfully controlled narratives of Mark Twain. When Stuart "talks" his story to us, we are very conscious of the presence of the speaker, most frequently a boy or a young man, who carries us through the various scenes of the tale. In keeping with this "talk style" is an almost exclusive use of the first-person point of view, so manipulated that it usually elicits a very high degree of empathy. Moreover, Stuart's beginning scenes are well contrived to intrigue the reader, to suck him into the stream of action which is in progress. He begins *in medias res* and tumbles the reader rapidly forward into whatever events the story is concerned with.

For instance, there is the beginning paragraph of "Another Hanging":

> I'll remember the Bellstrase Hangin' to my dyin' day. We've had our hangin's! We've had the Sizemore Hangin', the Dimmer Hangin', Dillmore Hangin', Perkins Hangin' and the Reeder Hangin'. We never had a hangin' that would come up to the Bellstrase Hangin' in 1903.
> It was one of the best hangin's this country has ever seen.[1]

After this joyous beginning, almost any reader would skim along to find the details of the memorable Bellstrase Hanging.

For that matter, who could resist following up the opening lines of "Love in the Spring"?

> It was last April when I met Effie. It was over at the Put-Off Ford at the Baptis foot-washing. Effie is a Slab Baptis. She was there having her feet washed. And I can't forget that day in April.[2]

Stuart has the gift of the natural storyteller, the knack of opening a story with a few brief lines that whet the reader's interest and at the same time embody very naturally the tone and mood of the story:

> "Where are we goin', Mom?" I said, looking up at my tall mother.
> "Where can we go when the moon is up and the lightning bugs are above the meadows?"[3]

So begins "Walk in the Moon Shadows," a story filled with the cool magic of an April night and a strange quest for two long-dead companions. The brief opening lines suggest the mystery and the magic of the story.

Even more important than these interesting, appealing openings is Stuart's style. Since his first-person narrator is usually a mountain boy of eastern Kentucky, he talks in a simple, straightforward manner—simple sentences with an occasional short compound sentence. Stuart is noted for his use of the dialect of his mountain region; but his use varies widely. In the story just cited, "Walk in the Moon Shadows," a young boy, Shan, is the narrator; and he tells a story in simple, clearcut, standard diction virtually free of dialect. When Stuart does use dialect, his usage is never extreme enough to obscure the reader's understanding. A few dialect words serve to give the flavor of the mountain speech: " 'Hit's that pretty little doll-baby over there tellin',' says Flora Bridgewater. 'That pretty little Rilda. I'll glomb them wax eyes from her pullet head.' "[4] "Glomb" in Stuart is almost always used in conjunction with "eyes" and always means "to scratch."

Particularly effective is the dialect in the story "Vacation in Hell": "I took th' big ripe peach and I cut drive at that spider's eyes. I took one o' 'em casouse."[5] The expression "cut drive," meaning "to strike without restraint," is an especially good one that seems to be confined to Stuart's region. "Casouse," meaning "to splash and splatter juicily," is a good, evocative onomatopoeic word. This entire story, "Vacation in Hell," is narrated in the first person by an untutored miner. His speech, flavored with dialect throughout, builds up a strong, compelling, and masculine narrative.

If we read all of Stuart's work, we come into possession of a rich supply of new dialect words and unusual idioms;[6] but Stuart's use of dialect is never self-conscious or condescending. He writes from within this speech tradition and conveys the life of his people—their thinking and their being—and, with great naturalness and conviction, he does it in their own speech and without obscurity. Words and phrases like "fittified," "fornenst," "gander around," "ol' coon cack," "golly-whopper," "a gone goslin," "hold your tater," "hunker," "jump the broom," "norrate," "poddlin," "quiled," "simlon head," "slonchways," and "vidaciously" appear throughout Stuart's writing in a natural, effective manner. The incidence of these dialect expressions does, however, seem to decline as we come to Stuart's later stories. Presumably in his early stories, which dealt frequently with events in the first years of the twentieth century, dialect reflected the actual speech custom. Radio, the automobile, and television have taken some of the color out of W-Hollow speech, a fact reflected in the diction of his later stories.

As important as dialect is Stuart's use of figurative language. We should expect a poet to make considerable use of metaphor in his prose; certainly Stuart does. Stuart writes a highly imagistic prose, full of visual and auditory images: "Uncle Uglybird climbed slowly up the little foxpath that wound like a snake up the steep bluff toward the ridge. . . . The August sun beamed from the sky like a white agate marble."[7]

Nature in all its concrete details plays constantly through the stories. The illustrative figures are those of a highly perceptive country man. Sometimes the style suffers from certain obsessive phrases: white oaks are, as we have noted, always "tough-butted white oaks," and the mountain men are usually "beardy men." Sometimes, and this is particularly true in his earlier stories, the style is marred by an excessive use of tropes, as if his poetic imagination had gotten completely out of control. The result is that the lyric flights divert us from the story, slow down the tempo, and throw it out of balance. Yet this is a minor flaw; in fact, some of his best stories result from the combination of a fast tempo with an exuberant lyricism.

An excellent example of this exuberant lyricism is the story "Another Hanging."[8] From the first paragraph—which begins, "I'll remember the Bellstrase Hangin' to my dyin' day," and ends, "It was one of the best hangin's this country has ever seen"— we are in a fast-tempoed, high-keyed comic narrative with a high-spirited boy relating all the fun of the hanging. Willard Bellstrase has cut the throat of Blaze Gullet, and the county is going to hang him for it. The school boys are all glad to get the news: "It kind o' tickled all of us when we heard about it. Tom, Big Aaron and Little Edd and Zulus—I wish you could a heard 'em. We'll get to leave school. We'll get to go home for the hangin'. It'll be the biggest hangin' we've had in many a day!' "[9] This note of callous joy is maintained by the speaker throughout the story: "Didn't care nary a bit when I heard old Willard was going to hang by the neck. It tickled me fer I thought he was gettin' what was comin' to 'im."[10]

Eif, the boy narrator, is mainly concerned with dressing up in loud clothes to show off before all his friends who will be at the hangin'. He buys a pair of high-heeled button shoes, a new hat, and a powder-blue double-breasted suit with peg-legs: "I'll show 'em who looks good and who don't." The train, a special excursion train for the hanging, comes puffing up about midnight to take the mad delirious mob on board:

> . . . the passengers were a-hollerin' like a lost flock of wild geese. Passengers were wavin' hankerchiefs—and the boys were standin' on the flatcars huggin' the girls. . . .Some of the boys were drunk as all getout and had their pistols out. Their sweethearts were hangin' on to their arms tryin' to get 'em to put their pistols in their pockets—a-cryin' and a-beggin' to 'em! Men were trying to fight on the train.[11]

Now begins a wild, delirious ride through the night, reminiscent in its poetic gusto of the famous train ride through Virginia in the opening of Wolfe's *Of Time and the River*. Stuart writes:

> I'll tell you a night in May with a lively crowd on the train and a hangin' almost in sight is wonderful! . . . It was one of the prettiest nights I ever saw in my life. No wonder boys and girls were lovin' on the train. . . . Right up the track, huffety-puffety,

huffety-puffety, and the smoke rolled in black rock-cliff mountains across the moon. . . . I was afraid the train would wreck
and I wouldn't get to see the hangin'. Then I'd take another
notion and think it would be great to be in a train wreck and roll
down from a cliff into the river—bumpety-bumpety—bumpety-
bumpety! Right over the cliffs into the river and the boys on the
flatcars a-goin' down through the air a-hollerin' and cavertin'
and the moonshine jugs, horse quarts and fruit jars flyin' in the
air.[12]

This complete, joyous abandon running all the way through
the story flings it forward with a rushing, roaring speed. Eif, the
narrator, feels no pity for the hanged man; Jesse Stuart does.
The flat unconcern of Eif and the crowd is balanced by a strong
undercurrent of pity on the part of the reading audience, pity
evoked by the very events cited without concern by Eif. Eif
shows us the condemned man in his cell and his wife and children outside the bars screaming at the top of their voices. Willard
Bellstrase is the helpless victim of this Saturnalia, and he has to
be sacrificed: " 'Bring on the man,' they screamed."[13]
At this point, Eif meets Beadie Blevins, "the prettiest girl at
the hangin'," and this combination of love and hanging makes
his happiness complete:

Willard's children were around the jail winders a-screamin'
and a-praying. Bertha Bellstrase was there a-screamin' till you
could a heard her across the mountain. I was the happiest young
man in the world. I was with my Beadie.[13]
The Bellstrases are there with their guns, but they cannot stop
the hangin'. The crowd is too big for them. We'd a had one of
the awfulest times there ever was after havin' the train to bring
people in from every place and then not have a hangin'. It
wouldn't've done. The people intended to see a hangin'.[14]
"Willard scooted and skived-up the grass cussed, hollered and
prayed," while the sheriff was getting him to the scaffold where
he "was goin' like a blind dog in a meat-house." The crowd
roars with laughter. " 'Ah, Buddie, how do you like your night-
cap?' some man hollered." Then it's time for Willard's confession.
The crowd wants it.
"I'd like to slit every damn Gullet's throat among these hills,"
Willard shouted. "The cowardly sons-of-bitches! Goddamn every
cowardly son-of-a-bitch and his brother among 'em! I'll show you
I can die like a man. . . . Let my life end! Just one time to die
and I'll soon get it over with! All I got to say is turn the button
and let the Goddamn trap fall."

> Screams roared from the crowd.
> "Take off that hood."
> "Let the Goddamn trap door fall!"
> "Let's see the Goddamn thing end."
>
> "This is a real hangin'," Beadie said. "It's the best hangin' I ever saw, Honey. I'm glad I come and met you."[15]

So they spring the trap; Willard drops through; and, as his body spins round and round, the crowd goes mad with joy! " 'Cut the rope and hang him again,' one man standing near us said. 'Grab up somebody and hang 'em.' " But all good things have to end: "Bertha fainted and her children took off to the weeds a-screamin'! It was getting about milkin' time now and the hangin' was over." The soberer people loaded the drunks on the Old Line Special, and it takes off with the mob fighting and shouting all the way back in the coaches, on top of the boxcars, and on the flatcars. " 'It's got so bad you just can't have a decent hangin' any more,' Beadie said. 'You are right, Honey,' I said. "My suit looks like it's never been pressed. . . .' I held Beadie in my arms and loved her all the way back to White Rock."

This comic gusto fills the story with Eif's deadpan exuberance, his joy at a whopping good social occasion. Just as certainly a vast irony fills the story as we note the huge unconcern of Eif and the mob to Willard Bellstrase's fate—their drunken carnival with death. One of Stuart's most potent and economical stories, it has poetry, humor, irony, and pathos in a multi-level structure. Reading it, we inevitably think of Mark Twain's irony in the Boggs shooting scene observed by Huck Finn. As good as Twain is in this scene, Stuart does not suffer by comparison. This comic gusto is certainly one of the dominant motifs in Stuart, and it is a very American brand of humor. Frequently it stretches out into the tall-tale humor of the old Southwest—into stories that George Washington Harris, creator of Sut Lovingood, would have loved to hear.

A touch of this tall-tale extravagance appears in the story "Betwixt Life and Death."[16] In December, Grandpa Grayhouse dies at ninety-six, having left strict instructions that his will be carried out to the letter. The troublesome provision of the will is the injunction that his body be left up in the garret and not buried until "the wild roses bloom again." Furthermore, his heirs are to "have a settin' up each Friday night," and all the young folks are to be invited in to dance and have fun. So Pap sets out to fulfill these instructions. Several barrels of salt are poured around Grandpa in his coffin, and the coffin is placed in the garret. The night "settins-up" become famous through the county and are attended by large numbers of young people, much to grandson George's delight.

George falls in love with Gracie Thombs and wishes that they could just keep Grandpa preserved in salt forever:

> Our settin' up didn't end until the moon went down in the mornin' and the roosters had started crowin'. I just wondered what Grandpa thought about the good times we's havin' now. I believe if Grandpa knowed how much better our good times was a-gettin' he wouldn't have been buried until summer was over—maybe not until snow fell again. I was havin' the best time I'd ever had in my life.[17]

But the good times must end; Grandpa, still perfectly preserved in salt, is brought down from the garret and buried as stipulated. Only a fist fight between George and his Cousin Willie over a girl mars the funeral.

This influence of the old Southwest is even more apparent in Stuart's story "Horse-Trading Trembles,"[18] in which Finn Tremble completely takes in sharp horse-trader Erf Sizemore by telling him the truth about a worthless horse in such a way that he, gulled by the truth, buys it. This trick is a faithful recapitulation of the one in A. B. Longstreet's "The Horse Swap," which appeared in *Georgia Scenes* (1835) and launched the nationwide popularity of this intensely American humor. Without consciously attempting to, Stuart perpetuates with great fidelity this racy, realistic humor.

Stuart picks up the tall-tale element in his story "Sylvania Is Dead."[19] Sylvania, a woman bootlegger of six hundred and fifty pounds, lives in a small shack on top of a high mountain plateau and purveys moonshine of a high quality to all dwellers of the surrounding mountains. Sylvania is so fat that, when the revenuers catch her, they cannot get her out of the house, much less off the mountain. So, as soon as they leave, she opens up a new keg; and the customers come out of the bushes. When she dies, all her erstwhile customers gather to help bury her; and it takes about all of them. They knock the chimney down and remove one end of the shack to get the coffin out. Twenty men hold on to the plowlines under the coffin to lower the huge weight into the grave. The mourners drink dipper after dipper from Sylvania's last barrel of moonshine and weep liquidly for their lost bootlegger. The extravagance and hyperbole of this story is characteristic of America's tall-tale humor and of much of Stuart's humor.

The reverse of this broad comedy is a kind of surrealistic or "Black Bile" humor in which we get the projection of the comic into the horrible with a strong element of exaggeration. Perhaps the most horrible of these stories is "Word and the Flesh,"[20] a grisly account of Brother Fain Groan, a religious fanatic, who sets off in the dead of night, clothed in a white gown and followed by six of his gullible disciples, to dig up the body of his wife from Kale Nelson Graveyard. They dig in the hot darkness and fall into a den of copperhead snakes on the dead woman's coffin. Four men are bitten and lie writhing about, vomiting and groaning, when the coffin is finally hoisted to the surface for Brother Groan to pry the top off. Brother Groan has brought with him his wife's clothing so she can change from her funeral garb and walk out of the graveyard with him. His faith in the Word is going to resurrect her.

When he gets the top off and strikes a match in the thick blackness, he sees the hairlipped face of his wife change from gray to poisonous black as the wind blows upon her: "My God Almighty. My wife. My God! Oh my God, but it is my wife. Perfectly natural too! My God!" Brother Groan falls dead beside the coffin, and the two disciples who are still able to walk flee from the sickening odor pouring out of the open coffin. Rescuers come next morning and discover crows and buzzards eating the faces of Brother Groan and his dead wife. Four snake-bitten men lie senseless in pools of sun-dried vomit. Constable Ricks arrests the body of the dead Brother Groan on the charge of "Public Indecency." Constable Ricks says, "My duties have been faithfully performed within the 'sharp eyes' of the law." Women fight over the clothes of Fain Groan's wife. The story ends with a quick look at two of the men who lost arms from the snakebites. A third has lost an entire jaw, and we see the food dribbling out of his jawless mouth as he eats. The fourth has only a bony end on one leg where the flesh had rotted off. A gruesome and grotesque story, it reminds one a great deal of Erskine Caldwell, with whom Stuart shares some striking similarities. Yet the surrealistic remains a minor motif in Stuart's humor.

Actually Stuart's humor is primarily a good-natured reveling in comic incongruities, which he depicts with great gusto and without any intent to harm or hurt. He laughs at the central figures of his human comedy but in a genial, understanding manner, as in "Uncle John, the Baptist,"[21] in which we meet beanpole Uncle John—a shouting Free Will Baptist who says he is "Six feet and seven inches tall. . . . Every inch a Free Willer and every inch the Lord's"— and Uncle John's wife, five feet tall and "Two hundred and sixty-five pounds of Baptist." This is Stuart's most typical vein of humor, and it ties in with the whole bent of his work—with his refusal to propagandize and slant his work to please the sociological critics dominant when he began writing.

There is a deep tenderness in Stuart, a great pity and love for people; and this quality shows through in his short stories as it does in his personal life. This tenderness appears in his poignant little story, "Thanksgiving Hunter,"[22] in which a young boy, out in the fields on his first dove hunt, is anxious to prove his prowess as a hunter. A pity for the beautiful birds falls on him, and he separates himself from the other hunters because he is sensitive to the great slaughter of birds. Finally, he thinks he will kill a dove to take back with him; and he calls one with the dove cry his uncle has taught him. When a dove flies to the rock beside him, trying to reach his call, the boy looks closely at it; it is blind; both eyes have been shot away: "Though it was blind, I couldn't kill it, and yet I knew it would have a hard time to live." Then the dove hears its mate's voice in the near-by trees and flutters painfully toward the sound: "I heard its wings batting the wind-shaken pine boughs as it ascended, struggling, toward the beckoning voice." And the story closes with the boy's sharp pain at the tongueless agony of life.

Stuart creates a fictional world of great charm and dramatic presence. It has solidity and depth and the authority of the specific detail rightly selected. In his best stories this world is dramatized completely; everything comes alive; and we can see and smell and feel all the weathers of W-Hollow as if we were actually walking through it. Even stories which have little overt action still convey this dramatic presence because of the sense of life, atmosphere, sound, and people which jingle on through them. "The Bellin of the Bride,"[23] for instance, conveys this kinetic, dancing sense of life throughout the story. The key to this dynamism and credibility lies in the reality of the narrative voice.

This complete realism of voice stance gives Stuart full authority of narration and establishes his fictional world with solid dimensions. The themes that emerge from this fictional world are not very complicated. First, life is hard for the Powderjays and the other dwellers in W-Hollow, as in "Dark Winter,"[24] in which a family with a bedfast father is caught by poverty and near starvation in a cold, cruel winter; or as in "Uncle Jeff,"[25] where Uncle Jeff dies in a city hospital after a long life of hard manual labor at poor pay, bedeviled in his last moments by the remembered amours of his second wife with various lovers. But in W-Hollow people endure the hardships of life and fight back; if they must go down, they go down resisting and kicking. This stoic endurance pays off, and they frequently win through to a victory or a half victory. "Dark Winter," for instance, ends with the painful death of the little infant son born during the bitter winter. When Stuart rewrote this story and called it "Spring Victory,"[26] he made the infant alive and well at the end of the story; and the family swells with the strong exuberance of spring life. " 'All our debts are paid, Mick,' Mom said. 'The hard winter is over. Violets are in bloom and pasture grass is coming back to the pastures.' "

Life is hard, but it is worth it. Stuart is an affirmer, a yea-sayer, in his short stories. Like Thoreau, he shows that life close to the bone is hard, but the taste is sweet. The pulse of life is sweet and wild and uncurbed in these dark hills. Gusto and vitality leap from the pages of "300 Acres of Elbow-Room,"[27] "Battle Keaton Dies,"[28] "Another April,"[29] "Grandpa Birdwell's Last Battle,"[30] and "Another Hanging."[31] This vitalism is more than a theme; it is really a mode of his fiction, and makes dramatic and activistic the simplest scene in Stuart's work. This is quite apparent in the climactic scene of "Dawn of Remembered Spring,"[32] where Shan Powderjay discovers two copperhead snakes locked motionless in a love embrace, and various mountain people come and watch and are slowly transfigured by this wonder, a wonder that is gradually transmitted to the reader— one of Stuart's memorable epiphanies.

Life is hard, one endures; but there are compensations along the way. Nature is one of the greatest compensations. The sounds, odors, and images of an outdoor world flow steadily through Stuart's pages. No other American writer of the twentieth century keeps us so constantly in an outdoor world. We feel it in this sentence—"My father can take a handful of new-ground dirt in his hand, smell of it, then sift it between his fingers and tell whether to plant the land in corn, tobacco, cane or potatoes."[33] The story "Clearing in the Sky"[34] becomes a kind of hymn to the agrarian world, as Jesse walks with his seventy year old father to a secret garden in a clearing on top of a mountain. When his father smells the rich, dark, leaf-rot loam, he says that in working this garden he is renewing his youth in the fertile, primeval soil—real land like God left it.

Beyond the delight of nature lies the bittersweet joy of remembered event, now long past. Ecclesiastes' lament for the bitter brevity of life, long a favorite of Stuart's, creeps into many of his stories of vanished scenes and people. Such a lament is "Huey, the Engineer,"[35] a story which becomes a kind of folk poem celebrating a little thirty-seven mile eastern Kentucky railroad which began in Grant's time and lasted till 1930. As the story junkets along, lost time and lost America stream by us in a pell-mell flow till the day Huey dies and the track is dug up. We stand with the narrator by Huey's coffin:

> But now—the silent hands . . . tears for our engineer that once pulled the train where no track now is—nothing but the wind and dents in the earth and cinders ground down and old bridges —but we remember—we'll always remember—and Huey—our engineer—we wonder on what silent train and to what silent land our engineer has gone.[36]

Equally important in the appeal of Stuart's work is the glimpse he gives us of the old, free, pastoral world of our fathers. Beset as we are by the jungle violence of deteriorating world-cities, by the nightmarish vision of hordes of mass-men held in fief to the Big Brothers of this world, we turn with relief and stern joy to the prickly, individual world of Mick Powderjay and Uglybird Skinner—to a nostalgic evocation of a vanished past. Yet Stuart is not a conscious propagandist of the good old days. He could have used his material for social propaganda as easily as Caldwell did and so have gained the favor of the sociological critics dominant in the 1930's. But with exceptions that number not more than five, he has refused to propagandize and slant his material.

In summary, Stuart is primarily a *maker*, a *poet*. He has a feeling for the life of things. He depicts things exactly and lets the universal shine through. He is the observer, the enjoyer—not the exhorter, the preacher. In this sense, he is a true artist. He digs deep into W-Hollow—shows and observes and wonders at it. Stuart says "Yes" to life all along the way in his short stories— "Yes" in spite of sickness, injustice, and death; "Yes" to the bone-deep sweetness and diversity of life. But he does not preach; he lets his world speak for itself. He has avoided literary cliques and coteries; he has swum alone. He has amassed his reputation as a short story writer slowly. His real and lasting reputation is still ahead of him.

CHAPTER 4

The Major Novels:
Children of the Earth

I *Introduction*

ACCORDING to Oscar Sammons, Stuart's long-time friend (and the model for Lawyer John Oscar Simmons who draws up the "ar-tickle" for Anse Bushman in *Trees of Heaven*), Stuart had talked about writing a novel but had done nothing about it. Oscar set out to needle Stuart about his all-talk and no-novel policy until Stuart in three months turned out his first novel, *Trees of Heaven,* while spending part of his time at the home of Oscar and Ann Sammons. Since then Stuart has published seven novels, including best-seller *Taps For Private Tussie.*

In an article in February, 1947, "How I Became a Novelist," in the *Author and Journalist,* Stuart gives a slightly different version of his debut as a novelist: he returned from his Guggenheim travels in Europe and decided to try a novel because the news release on his return said he had brought back a novel manuscript with him (which was not true). In any case, he did set to work in August, 1939, cutting "sprouts" in the field by day and writing the novel by night. When the "sprouts" got to be too much for him, he moved into town, courted Naomi Deane Norris, married her, and finished the manuscript five days later in an abandoned room of the court house—a room distinguished by falling plaster and a fretting of yellow jackets' nests. He borrowed a hundred dollars and set out for New York to sell the novel. E. P. Dutton and Company took it, paid him a two hundred and fifty dollars advance, and launched him on his novel-writing career.

Before considering this first novel, we should note some of Stuart's general characteristics as a novelist. Like Wolfe, Stuart thinks of himself as a *writing man.* Like Wolfe, he sees no great distinction between fiction and autobiography; he slides easily from one to another. He has seen and experienced certain things which have marked him strongly, and he delights in writing about them. Because the physical act of writing is a real pleasure to him, he writes prodigiously and may do so all night. He has written millions of words; he wants to be published; he wants people to read him; but, if they ceased to read his work, if he could no longer get published, he would write anyway. He has a compulsion to construct verbal pictures of the people he has seen and known and all the varying weathers that have steeped W-Hollow since 1906. Substituting Asheville, North Carolina, for W-Hollow we could make all the above statements with equal validity about Thomas Wolfe. We can comprehend Stuart as a novelist more clearly if we see his similarity to Wolfe.

The central fact about Stuart as a novelist is that he has created a spacious, complex, imaginative world by projecting the actual one of W-Hollow onto an imaginative plane, and there he lives and has his imaginative being. This world becomes a kind of vast continuum realized with equal validity in his poems, short stories, autobiographies, biography, and novels. His imagination plays over this world constantly, and he walks about with a head full of scenes, episodes, and characters which eventually precipitate themselves into stories, novels, and essays. The bridge that carries the world of W-Hollow over into Stuart's novels is the Stuart short story. His novels are, in many ways, prolongations of his short stories into a more spacious esthetic scope. *Taps For Private Tussie* and *Hie to the Hunter* were both begun as short stories, became too long, and were recast and expanded to novel length.

Like his short stories, his novels have a kind of subconscious plot; for Stuart is not the Jamesian practitioner of the well-made novel. He never outlines a book except for a few notes which may be sketched out on an envelope. He has some image, some "hunch," some node of interest in his own mind which is the real subject matter of the novel, and his characters begin to come alive and dance their attitudes around this node of interest, shaping a fable which may mean something quite contrary to Stuart's original intent. Novel structure for him is expressed in a metaphor; for he visualizes, he says, the structure of a story as a range of mountains. His central character is the highest, most massive ridge, and the minor figures are the connecting foothills radiating out from the dominant ridge. This metaphor gives him a kind of perspective on the relationship of his characters to one another, one which he tries to maintain throughout the entire novel.

We can use still another analogy about Stuart as a novelist. He is, in a manner of speaking, the Grandma Moses of the novel. That is, he is a kind of "primitive" also. He uses strong, stark scenes clearly and sharply delineated. His style is simple and direct to the point of crudity. He has a superlative sense of the "folk" and a feeling for their joy and their concerns. He paints a world that is now lost and gone to us, about which hangs an air of rusticity and nostalgia which accounts for much of its charm. Like Grandma Moses, Stuart in his most successful novel, *Taps For Private Tussie,* employs the vision of a child to render the world for us—a world seen clearly and precisely in sharp detail. As is the case with Grandma Moses, the poetry of the earth is never dead for Stuart, and he writes lovingly and in detail about the weathers and nights and days of nature in W-Hollow. Some of Grandma Moses' paintings could be called visual ballads, and some of Stuart's novels could be called prose ballads; we get a strong lyrical quality in both.

In trying to get at Stuart's quality, we should consider also a certain affinity with Dickens. Dickens characterizes obviously and bluntly, using name typing (Mr. Murdstone), a characterizing mannerism or gesture (Uriah Heep's ritual wringing of his hands repeated whenever he comes on stage). Like Dickens, Stuart uses name-typing, collects grotesque and unusual names from tombstones in Plum Grove Churchyard (Uncle Sweeter Dabney, Horsefly Salyers, Hootbird Hammertight), and employs the characterizing gesture (Grandpa Tussie's amber spittle and the back of his hand across the stained whiskers), is fascinated by oddities and eccentrics ("Old Glory" Gardner, gone nuts on the flag, and Temperance and Ollie Spradling, an alcoholic couple who demonstrate *caritas* by having Temperance knock Ollie down until he can no longer arise). Stuart's style like Dickens' is dramatic, kinetic, bustling with dialogue and action. Instead of *telling,* he *shows.* He loves the present tense. It is more dramatic, immediate, objective—it's happening right there before you now. But his style is far simpler than that of Dickens; Stuart creates a "talk-style" simple and direct—rarely using a word longer than two or three syllables.

Stuart cannot be categorized as a Realist or as a Romantic; he fits comfortably in neither category. There is Realism enough in his work: the dialect is sharp and authentic; the customs and habitudes of W-Hollow are closely observed and dramatized; and the characters are, for the most, part living credible beings. Yet there is a Romantic streak running through his novels, a kind of Romantic primitivism, for instance, in his treatment of nature and in his idealization of Grandpa Tussie in the latter stages of *Taps For Private Tussie.* The Romantic motif of the child as seer occurs frequently in his work, as does his Romantic idealization of the simple people of this world. Stuart does not have to be labeled; but, if some one insists on doing it anyway, we should best call him a regionalist who mingles the modes of Romanticism and Realism in his work. How he does this can readily be seen in his first novel, *Trees of Heaven.*

II Trees of Heaven

The basic plot of *Trees of Heaven* can be stated very quickly: Patriarch Anse Bushman loves the land and wants to own more of it. The gospel he preaches is work—work always and be thrifty and the reward will be more land. And what greater joy could a man possess this side of heaven? For that matter, how could heaven itself offer a greater joy—heaven will be less for Anse unless he can set his plowshare in heavenly soil and plow a straight furrow. Conflict arises when Anse's wife Fronnie and his youngest son, Tarvin, oppose him and aver that he is ruining everybody's life with his overweening gospel of work.

The conflict is increased when Tarvin falls in love with Subrinea Tussie, the beautiful daughter of Boliver Tussie, head of a family of squatters who represent indolence personified—everything, in fact, that Anse excoriates. For a few months, through Tarvin's interposition, the Tussies are sharecroppers on Anse's land, having signed an iron-clad and puritanical "artickle" that Anse has drawn up prohibiting them from frolicking, moonshining, dancing, attending revivals, and having babies. The Tussies, who turn out to be hard workers, have a fine crop going when Anse suddenly discovers that they are moonshining on his land, have run up a four hundred dollar grocery bill charged to him, and are going to have *two* babies, one being Subrinea's, sired by Anse's boy, Tarvin. At this news, seventy year old Anse blows higher than the Krakatoa volcano. He sails into court and gets the Tussies thrown off his land. He tries to break up Subrinea and Tarvin; failing, he grudgingly agrees to their staying on his land. At this point Anse providentially is struck on the head by a falling tree limb.

A long coma ensues during which he has a "token"—a vision of himself in hell. Awaking from the coma a new man, he instructs Tarvin to bring the Tussies back and to give them their house and share of the crop; Anse will no longer oppose them. The novel ends with Tarvin driving his wagon into town to bring the Tussies back; as he does so, he is thinking that in spite of all the human tensions the earth endures forever, and that he and Subrinea will have the earth and the endless cycle of seasons and "there will be the winy sunlight coming again tomorrow."[1]

It may seem strange to say that Anse Bushman is a theme, but in a sense he is. The novel is largely *about* Anse Bushman. He is a *primary* character; the other characters are subordinate to him, and more or less come to life only as they are in some way affected by or respond to him. Obviously Anse intrigued Stuart, and he devotes more space to Anse than to any other character. We have, therefore, to get into the heart of Anse to read the core of the novel.

To begin with, Anse is a splendid animal. He is seventy years old, but as strong as the mules he works and babies, and as tough as the rocky hills he lives among. He has strong, primitive appetites. He loves food and the physical act of eating: "I'd ruther watch hogs eat . . . as to eat myself . . . Watch them white hogs try to lay down in the trough, won't you? I like to see 'em greedy like that. I like to see a person eat like a hog. I'm jealous of a man that can eat more than I can. . . . I've allus had an appetite like a hog fer I've allus worked like a brute" (p. 40). But stronger than Anse's appetite for food is his love for the land. He loves it physically: ". . . digging into the earth, lifting handfuls of dirt up and examining them carefully, rubbing dirt between his bare hands, smelling it, and fondling it as Subrinea fondles the lambs" (p. 129). Like a modern Antaeus, his strength courses up from the land: "Anse feels the strength of youth as he walks over the furrowed earth. Anse can feel strength in his bare feet as he puts them back to earth and walks slowly" (p. 263).

The land is his dream, the vision he lives by: "I've got my mind made up what I aim to do as soon as I git that land. I aim to conquer it as I have conquered this. Look at this land, Tarvin. Look how purty it is to the far hilltop yonder beyond the house. . . . I want to git that big timber tract in shape if I buy it. I want to put it in shape as the last job I do on this earth" (pp. 46-47). This dream is the most beautiful one Anse can imagine. Later, as he sits before the fire with Fronnie, he dreams of the big farm he will have with hundreds of sheep and cattle in the velvety knee-deep grass, of the smell of the loamy earth and of the feel of the earth in his hands. "Anse dreams more than a young man dreams and he plans at the age of seventy to go on living forever and forever" (p. 134).

As a result of this singleminded dream, Anse has driven his children so hard that he and Fronnie end with only Tarvin left to them. Of eleven children, five have died; five have flown the nest, and none write, not even at Christmas time. Yet Anse has become the tough, red-bearded patriarch of the community: "He is the patriarch, the man that cannot make a mistake in the community, the man whose words everybody must listen to, the man whose big farm and whose reputation for hard work and thrift have earned him an enviable place in the community" (p. 66). Anse is a patriarch who loves the outdoors so much that he cannot stay indoors when the great spring equinoctial storms come. He plunges out into the night and walks unprotected up and down his fields, soaking up the water, thunder, and lightning and thinking, "A sight like this will only come once. . . . This is the resurrection of spring. . . .Tomorrow we will have a new earth. . . . This is the best night of the year" (p. 220).

All the other characters shrink when placed beside Anse. He has faults—is stubborn, opinionated, drives his workers relentlessly, but he comes alive with unquestioned authenticity as an earthy, elemental, sensuous, strong, and domineering man. In drawing the character of Anse, Stuart must have relied greatly on the character of Mitch Stuart, who possessed all of Anse Bushman's good characteristics—such as his love of land—and some of his stubbornness. Anse's threshing about in the throes of his passion keeps the novel moving and breeds the necessary tensions until he is clubbed over the head by a falling tree. Stuart, who likes and admires him, uses him to put iron in the theme (one of the major ones in the book) that life is hard in the hills. After Anse has worked a man, the man knows that life is hard.

Fronnie and Tarvin continually stress this stoic theme. Tarvin works at the cane mill until he staggers: "I'm all pooped out, Ma. . . . Pa has nearly worked me to death. . . . Pa puts his money into the land. . . . He puts my work into the land. All of my strength goes back into the land. The land is all" (p. 55). Fronnie listens sympathetically, then lifts a contrapuntal complaint: "If you ever marry, Tarvin . . . don't ever let your wife work like I haf to work. I've had to work like this and carry you youngsters. . . . I've throwed my hoe down in the cornfield and went to the house to have my baby. . . . You was born in the cornfield. I couldn't get to the house in time" (p. 56).

Even the carefree Tussies are unable to escape the continuous attrition of life in the hills. We see Boliver Tussie going in to Anse's house to sign the abhorred "ar-tickle": "Boliver's shoulders are slightly rounded by heavy lifting. Deep lines have started grooving his face. It has happened too soon for his years" (p. 110). Or Tarvin looks at his mother again and again, as Stuart must have looked at his mountain mother, and wondered: "I jest look at Ma going around in shoes without stockings on her legs. I see the big clumps of blood showing under the skin in the broken veins. I see the strain of toil on her face. I jest wonder if life is worth livin when a woman hast to work like Ma has had to work" (p. 113). Men and women break early in the mountains under the strain of all they have to endure.

Life is hard both for the owners (the Bushmans) and the squatters (the Tussies) in this mountain milieu, but the squatters have one way out. They follow Boliver Tussie's way of life: "If I didn't have me a little snort from the jug every Saturday, life wouldn't be worth living. Jest a little snort from the jug on Saturday and fox huntin' two nights out of the week and something to eat three times a day, good homemade twist to chaw, and old Boliver can git along in this world" (p. 25). Tarvin, aching from the hardness of his father's endless labor, looks on the Tussie way with favor and mediates the two points of view. He likes their frolicking, moonshining, hunting, and dancing. He warns Anse Bushman that the Tussies cannot be put under a yoke: "They have the same wildness in their blood and flesh as you have found in new-ground. You've got to work easy with the Tussies" (pp. 297-98). And this *carpe diem* theme, rippling all the way through the novel, washes over tough old Anse and eventually brings him to terms.

There is a hint of death-in-life in these dark mountains, but there is a resurrection too. Over and over again in this book (as in his poems in *Album of Destiny*), Stuart voices the joy of resurrection. His characters never tire of looking at the dying vegetation of fall, or at the dead vegetation of winter, seeing in their mind's eye the new life of spring. As November comes, the choral voice of the omniscient narrator intones: "Life has left the hills. The trees have gone into the sleep of death—that sleep of an awaited resurrection. . ." (p. 92). Tarvin, who pauses on a ridge in the midst of a bitterly cold snow storm, looks at the frozen sprouts and trees—sleeping the sleep of death. We hear his thoughts: "Their resurrection . . . will be in the spring. They will leaf again and blossoms will come to their boughs . . . All of my youth has been winter. When I met Subrinea it was spring" (pp. 102-3). March approaches with its subtle atmosphere changes—so like winter, yet to a knowing outdoorsman like Anse, different. He sniffs the sharp air.: "I can smell the spring in these woods. I can smell the land waiting to be plowed. I can smell the livin' roots workin' under the moldering leaves" (p. 164). Anse and Tarvin both long for the life-returning sign of the first March thundershowers. Tarvin speaks for them both when he says that the equinoctial storms are "the trumpet that wakes the livin' spring from its long winter sleep" (p. 198).

In a sense this resurrection motif can be considered a variant facet of the great nature theme which rolls throughout the novel and makes it a hymn to nature. The giant cyclical sweep of the year is measured by tobacco cutting in the fall; the autumnal harvest of sugar cane, the pressing of sorghum, stripping tobacco; winter with its lambing chores; spring with burning tobacco beds; early summer with tobacco planting and weed hoeing in the growing corn and tobacco. In this outdoor world, we feel time passing to natural rhythms. Occasionally, we are made aware through nature of the ancient mutability theme, as when Tarvin stands looking at the meadows frozen black in February's chill and thinks about ". . . this strange passing of time, marked only by the washing of new gulleys, the decaying of leaves and the slithering of frozen rocks" (p. 136).

In his first novel, Stuart was feeling his way along in the

thematic variations we have discussed—variations which for the most part appear in a modified form in poems and short stories published before *Trees of Heaven* appeared—and in narrative technique. The transition from short story to novel was a big one, but he tried to stick to his successful short-story techniques as much as possible. He uses, for instance, the present tense throughout most of the novel. The reader is listening to a third-person narrator who is omniscient in his ability to view the inner thoughts of all his characters. Stuart likes lots of dialogue and action; we thus get many dramatic presentations where the characters are conversing with each other or soliloquizing. Occasionally, the voice of the omniscient narrator becomes a chorus, giving us the great sweep of nature through the story or showing the pageant-like procession of characters, as they move off into the night from the sorghum-making frolic; then it changes to a pragmatic chatter as it tells the reader how to do things.

Stuart is fascinated by the process of doing things, and he is continually telling the urban reader how to do all sorts of farm jobs. Among other things the reader learns from *Trees of Heaven* how to press sugarcane, how to make sorghum molasses, how to kill hogs and render lard, how to burn new ground and plant tobacco (and how to worm, sucker, cut, house, strip, and cure it), how to skin a groundhog, and how to care for new-born lambs.[2] This passion for fact leads him to include a page and a half of the exact text of a mountain real estate deal with all of its legal and surveyor's jargon, plus three pages of an itemized grocery bill, reminiscent of Thoreau's itemized expense account in *Walden*.

Stuart's style, for the most part, is an extremely simple one and at times—as is true with Hemingway, also—he seems to parody himself. A kind of stylistic primitivism runs riot in the following excerpt:

> Tarvin laughs at Subrinea. He carries the hoe across his shoulder. His strong bronze face looks down at her tall body and her pretty face that looks up at him. Subrinea is swinging her basket along as she walks. She looks at Tarvin. She does not look where she steps. They walk down the hill from Subrinea's shack. They cross the creek under the poplar grove. They cross a little bottom. They walk under the thin-leafed beech trees and cross the creek again. They walk over the dark earth where the charcoal piles used to be. They walk down to the cliffs. (p. 228)

Doubtless Stuart would maintain that he is constructing a simple style to go with simple people, but this type of style led Hemingway to mock Sherwood Anderson's overdone simplicity in *Torrents of Spring*. Stuart matures and moves away from the oversimplicity in his later novels.

Along with this simple, direct, noun-verb style is the technique of closing each scene with a cinematic fade-out: "Boliver walks in front. He walks down the bank from the newground tobacco field. Crissie follows Boliver, and the children follow Boliver. Their bare feet walk silently over the dark muddy earth. They swing their arms as they walk down the path. . . . The stars have come into the sky. The wind is getting cool. A bull-bat flies over them and screams. A whippoorwill calls to its mate" (p. 238). This verbal equivalent of a cinematic fade-out has a highly visual quality, and we can hear the mood music swelling up as the Tussies disappear from view down the path.

Stuart attains variety and color of style through the use of colloquialisms and striking idioms that are integral to his narration. Tarvin, getting ready to knock out Bollie Beaver, declares—"I'll salivate him" (p. 65). Anse circulates four jugs of moonshine to the men at the sorghum making: "They hike and spit and drink" (p. 76). Subrinea saves Tarvin from a tempestuous blizzard and observes as he warms himself before the fire, "You come in one of getting lost" (p. 107). A widow seeing her land sold for taxes voices her rising anger: "I feel the Old Scratch [the devil] start at my navel and walk up to my throat" (p. 157). Fronnie, hearing about the two Tussie women who are trying to seduce Anse, is strongly vexed: "I hate the old gallivantin', lowdown strollops" (possibly a portmanteau word for "strumpet" and "trollop") (p. 249).

Often these idioms are articulated through old folk sayings or outlandish metaphors and thus gain even more vigor. When Bollie Beavers, for instance, threatens Anse, Anse warns the Sheriff. "If he molests me, I'll kill him dead as four o'clock. . . ." After Tarvin lays out Bollie Beaver with one blow at the dance, an old codger looking on says, "People ain't lost the color of their blood yet" (that is, haven't lost their courage) (p. 70). Anse, contemplating the agonizing possibility of having squatters as neighbors remarks to Fronnie, "I'd as soon be in hell with my back broke. . . ." (p. 38). When the sheriff arrests a grumbler at the land sale in the court square, the grumbler curses him:

"Handcuff me, you son-of-a-bitch. . . . you ain't gitting no virgin. I've been in your goddamn jail before" (p. 157). One of her children steals Crissie Tussie's chewing tobacco, and Crissie flings out a sharp warning: "If I find out the youngin that got my terbacker, . . . I'll stand him on his head and pour a bucket of water in his touch-hole" (pp. 250-51).

This crisp language moves the story along with wiry touches of humor. Stuart's style at its best is natural, concrete, moving—the key to a great part of his charm as a writer; but his is the proper style to emanate from the folk and to express the folk. The reader feels in reading *Trees of Heaven* that the author is not a self-conscious local-colorist preening himself on the quaintness of the folk, but an authentic artist sprung from their midst. Part of the folk atmosphere is evoked by the use of folk songs known to Stuart in his own childhood. The two Tussie boys, reclining on the ground, sing "Darlin' Cora," which begins:

> Darlin' Cora, Darlin' Cora,
> Come lay your hand in mine,
> You'll live a lady's life
> Long as the sun may shine.

The song runs on for four more stanzas about Cora's amorous misadventures and concludes with this stanza:

> The last time I saw Darlin' Cora
> She was sittin' on the bank by the sea
> With a big forty-four around her waist
> And a banjo on her knee. (pp. 20-21)

Later in the novel, when the invited guests stream down the hollow toward the big dance and sorghum-making, they sing their own version of "Down in the Valley, Valley So Low," which concludes with a local reference:

> Write me a letter, send it by mail,
> Send it in care of Greenupsburg jail;
> Greenupsburg jail, Love. Greenupsburg jail,
> Send it in care of Greenupsburg jail. (p. 62)

Once the dance starts Subrinea calls the sets, starting with a dance "Cage the Bird":

> Bird hops out and the crow hops in,
> All hands up and gone again.
> Move, children, move! Move, children, move!
>
> Change left hand lady, left hand around,
> Partner by the right and go whirly-giggin' 'round. (p. 72)

Fronnie requests the "Grapevine Twist" dance: "Join hands and circle down south, / Git that sunshine in your mouth" (p. 73). When this dance runs its course, Boliver Tussie requests, "that good old 'Figure Eight' dance."

> Jump up high and come down straight,
> Sixteen hands and circle eight,
> Circle eight when you git straight,
> Knock down Sal and pick up Kate. (p. 78)

The use of this folk element gives a diversity of interest to the novel—as does the note of humor which emerges from time to time. Humor is, however, not a major mode as it is in *Taps For Private Tussie;* it is incidental to the themes already discussed. A frontier type of humor, it appears in Boliver Tussie's lecture on the merits of drinking "pizen moonshine" which brought the buzzards low over his house waiting for him to kick the bucket and, says Crissie, "larnt him a lesson." "He watches the moonshine he drinks now" (p. 98).

Humor shows up in the entire court scene when Anse sues to get Boliver Tussie off of his land. The scene, conceived satirically throughout, depicts a dirty courtroom and an ignorant and venal judge whose prime recommendation as a jurist is that "Judge Whittlecomb has one of the finest pair of legs of any man in Kentucky" (p. 305). The judge spits on the floor and indifferently reads the racing records as the trial goes forward. Behind the judge hang pictures of Washington, Lincoln, Wilson, and Theodore Roosevelt, vainly promising "justice" to all.

The frontier humor also shows in the account of the fight between the North Fork boys and the Allcorn Creek boys at the Raccoon Church. "'They even pulled the seats up from the churchhouse floor,' says Kim Grace, 'and throwed 'em at each other. . . . Wimmen was fainting all over the church-house. Jest one boy got knifed. Boys didn't use powder and lead. That is one thing that can be said fer the boys. They's nice about that. They jest used the butts of their pistols, and knocked each other cold as cucumbers. I guess there's forty boys in that fracas. Got so anymore you can't go to the Lord's house on Sunday night and be safe'" (p. 303).

Putting the novel down and looking back over it, the reader becomes aware that it has certain deficiencies. The style becomes overly simple at times and parodies itself. There are passages where too much expository matter slows the dialogue. Anse's conversion, which is a big scene, is not convincing, even though the reader has been led to expect it; and it considerably weakens the ending. The lesser characters are not adequately developed; they all need to borrow some of Anse's vast vitality. There could have been some shortening and tightening of the novel to improve its tempo.

Moreover, there has been some dissatisfaction expressed by critics with the use of trees of heaven as a symbol. When Tarvin and Subrinea meet under the grove of trees of heaven, it is not only their place for love but also a graveyard in which the Tussie dead are buried—over a hundred Tussie graves are here. The trees of heaven, then, are intended to symbolize love and death, death and rebirth, the endless cycle of life as nature divulges it. The trees of heaven are considered a worthless wood by the lumbermen; it is too soft, and they say it is good only for firewood to feed the sawmill boiler. The worthlessness may allude to that of the shiftless Tussies. But as Subrinea says ". . . it's good to smell and it's purty to look at" (p. 32). In a way, then, the trees of heaven seem also to suggest the beauty of Subrinea sprung from the shabbiness of the Tussie clan. The image is a good one, and it does have some complexity of symbolic elaboration. All in all, it is difficult to fault Stuart here.

But the reader, of course, becomes aware of many excellences in the novel. Principally, I suppose, he is aware of a rich, fictional mountain world, one with various axes of interest. There are, for instance, the following: the love story of Subrinea and Tarvin, the conflict of squatter versus landowner, the pragmatic interest in learning how to do all sorts of farm processes, and the cycle and procession of seasons. These axes cut across one another and eventually fuse in a very satisfying representation of a now vanished mountain way of life. The reader will certainly be aware of Anse, who bestrides the entire world of *Trees of Heaven*, for Anse comes tumultuously alive. The reader will be aware of night and day, fog and rain, buzzards and snakes, and of all the sensuous paraphernalia of the outdoor world. He is aware of the unique idiom, the good earthy talk, and the light background of humor. He can taste the rich flavor of this mountain world.

All in all, the excellences well outweigh the deficiencies. *Trees of Heaven* is a good example of what Stuart is really writing in all the things he does—a hymn to earth.

III Taps For Private Tussie

Taps For Private Tussie (1943) quickly proved itself a favorite of the public. Within a couple of years, it had sold over a million copies. According to Stuart, it began as a short story which got too long; and, at the suggestion of his wife, he turned it into a novel. He has given some information on the genesis of the story. At an autographing party celebrating the publication of the novel, Stuart said he got the idea of *Taps For Private Tussie* in 1940: "The idea of people banding together to eat, to sing, just to be together fascinated me. I was taken with what people isolated could get from one another. I wrote this novel from the first to the last page. With *Trees of Heaven* I wrote the ending first."[3] Stuart said he wrote the novel as "a sad thing"; but, when his wife read it, she "cackled." Stuart wrote a first version of the ending in which Private Tussie remained dead and in a new one brought him back to life. The publishers preferred this second version—the one we now have.

Since much of Stuart's material comes from actual life, he often experiences a curious overlap between fiction and reality. For instance, there is an actual family of Tussies living in Greenup County. Stuart adopted the Tussie name instead of the real name of the family he used as prototypes. He records that, when the novel appeared and was sweeping the nation as a wartime best seller, Leslie's Drugstore in Greenup filled its window with copies of the novel. Stuart stopped one morning before the window to examine the display and was joined by one of the Tussies notorious for his indolence. This Tussie, who had never read the book—in fact, he had never read any book—looked with disgust at the display and finally observed sourly to Stuart, whom he didn't recognize, "Don't it beat all, the things a man will do to make a living." "People who don't read," says Stuart, "have really got confused on this and think I've used the Tussies and the Tussies think so too. But it was another family that served as the prototype."[4]

At first glance, *Taps For Private Tussie* seems artless and ingenuous. At second glance, we sense a kind of inner form. The story functions, for instance, as a comic ballad, a folk narrative with a strong lyric element and with various forms of incremental repetition. The narration has the simplicity and lack of self-consciousness normally ascribed to the ballad. There is also a kind of pageant character to the book, as in the scenes of the Tussies on the road or of the great clan of Tussies dancing through the night. In another sense the book acquires form from a great upward stroke of accretion followed by a downward plunge of loss. The ending modulates to a new movement of accretion with the appearance of Kim, who is to replace Grandpa as the new leader of the Tussies.

A look at the plot makes this pattern clearer. The novel begins with the burial of the Tussies' soldier son, Private Kim Tussie, who has been killed in the World War II. Kim's G.I. insurance money enables the Tussies to move out of the one-room schoolhouse which they have inhabited (and wrecked) into the Rayburn house, the finest in town. They buy new furniture for every one of the fourteen rooms, move in, and discover for the first time the wonders of an indoor toilet. The Tussies began with nothing and suddenly through Kim's death they begin to acquire things—a house, new clothes, fine furniture, good food, and new friends. The word gets around that Grandpa Tussie has struck it rich, but this new Utopia doesn't last long—soon the locusts begin to settle in the fine, big house.

First comes Uncle George, Grandpa's brother. A couple of days later Ben Tussie and his wife and three children knock and demand to be made a part of the new Tussie riches. Then the heavens open, and it rains Tussies until there are forty-six mouths to feed; Grandpa has no more space and is forced to turn away the other importunate Tussies, who depart cursing and vilifying him. Since none of the Tussies will work, they give themselves up to an idyllic existence of eating, sleeping, drinking Toodle Powell's bootleg liquor, and dancing all night long.

Utopia ends when Rayburn and the sheriff arrive, view the ruins of the once fine house, and throw everyone out; for by now the insurance money is gone. The expulsion from the house marks the end of the rhythmical upward movement of accretion. From this point on there is a falling movement as everything is taken away from the Tussies. Not only are house and money, but relief food and grocery account are lost, as are their fair-weather friends. Turned out on the road with no place to go, the Tussies are reduced to an abandoned shack in the winter-time with no food. When Uncle Mott kills two Tussie relatives, he is killed himself by Uncle George, who then sits in the shack with Mott's dead body and Grandpa's dying carcass—the lowest point of movement in the entire novel.

Next comes a rhythmic upturn of the novel as Kim suddenly reappears and reveals that Sid had known all along that the buried corpse was not that of Kim, but Sid wanted the life in-surance money. The novel ends with Kim rejoined to his wife Vittie. Kim tells Sid, the first-person boy narrator, that Vittie is Sid's mother. So Sid acquires a mother and a foster father; and it is implied that Kim will now head the Tussies, replacing the dying Grandpa, and will bring food and good times back to Sid, Grandma, and Vittie. The novel ends on a note of life affirma-tion when Sid says in the last sentence of the story ". . . I felt life surge through my body and I felt warmth from the big fire" (p. 303).

Kenneth Burke has remarked that in a primitive sense a lit-erary work can be considered "the dancing of an attitude." In *Taps* the basic attitude danced is a *sad-funny* one; that is, we have a surface comedy running all of the way through the book while we are treating very somber events (murder, deceit, wife-stealing). This peculiar mixture of comedy and pathos is cer-tainly part of the inner form of the book and gives it much of the charm which caught the public. Equally important to the inner form of this book was Stuart's choice of the boy, Sid Tussie, as the first-person narrator. Of the various personae Stuart has employed as his narrative voices, the boy narrator has been his most successful—witness Shan Powderjay, the narrator of so many of Stuart's more successful short stories. It is difficult to think of any other narrative mode which could provide Sid's combination of sympathetic insight into the foibles and virtues of the Tussies and evaluative comments on the character of these people. Probably the easiest way to bring Sid Tussie before the reader unfamiliar with him is to say that the ghost of Huck Finn walks through the pages of *Taps,* for Sid is like Huck Finn. Of course, each is a young unlettered boy and first-person narrator, and the parallels multiply. Each is a waif—an orphan—in some way isolated, alienated from a portion of his world. Sid, reared by the Tussies, finds that he has no Tussie blood in him; but he loves Grandpa Tussie who functions as a kind of father to him. But Grandma Tussie is not a mother to him—she kisses Sid only once in the course of the entire novel and does so because Sid has found and brought back to her all the old dishes and pans thrown away when they were flush with Kim's insurance money. Nor is Vittie a mother to him; and when Kim finally announces that Vittie is his mother, Sid's reaction is a singularly cool one. "It's hard for me to believe, I thought, but I didn't say anything. I'll never be able to call her 'Mother'" (p. 296). And not just surprise makes Sid say this; his own feeling is that Vittie has never shown him the least semblance of a mother's affection. Even Grandpa Tussie, who loves Sid, overlooks him when Uncle George appears on the scene for the first time and is meeting all the Tussie family: "I waited for Grandpa to introduce me but he didn't notice me" (p. 88).

With both Huck and Sid we have the child as seer. Alienated and alone, they tend to see people as they really are, not as they pretend to be. Huck gives us a clear view of the King and the Duke, and Sid shows us Uncle Mott as he really is, in contrast to the prettied up version presented by Grandma. Sid shows us Grandma calling Vittie "Honey" as long as she has the insurance money. Then he relates how Grandma turns on Vittie and tosses her out of the house as soon as her money is gone. Both boys see through sham, but they are not harsh judges. Each has a tender-hearted quality about him. Huck displays this in his famous decision to go to hell rather than give Jim back to slavery and in his pity for the villainous King and Duke when he sees them tarred and feathered. Sid, equally thin-skinned, gives up trapping: "I'll not trap again next year; I can't stand to kill little animals for their skin" (p. 253).

Uncle Mott is a kind of Pap Finn on a lesser scale, just as troublous in his cups, and he is in his cups just as frequently as he can find money to put him there. "There was Uncle Mott plain for us to see in front of the car, pitchin' headlong into the dust, gettin' up again and takin' in both sides of the turnpike" (p. 57). Sid's opinion of Uncle Mott is pretty much that of the new judge who set out to reform Pap Finn and put him up for the night in his best bedroom. That night Pap Finn woke up feeling dry and got himself a jug of forty-rod, and the next morning the judge had to take soundings to get through the room. The judge had enough of Pap Finn. Sid had enough of Uncle Mott.

Stuart is the only contemporary writer who can use the idiom of Huck Finn without being self-conscious or plagiaristic. Sid describes the life of the Tussies in the one-room school house: "Uncle Mott made music on his five-string banjer. It was a big floor. We just moved the seats back and had big times" (p. 36). "And had big times" is a genuine suspiration from the voice of Huck Finn, as all devotees of this Mississippi pariah will acknowledge. Throughout the novel Sid's vernacular narration is clear, boyish, not too heavily dialectal; it catches perfectly the persona of the boy narrator as Huck Finn catches it for Mark Twain. Any good work of art mingles many excellences; and, as we search for the topmost one in *Taps For Private Tussie,* it is this mastery of "sound posture" that we find to be its best single quality.

The more we look at Sid and Huck the more we feel this unintended parallelism. Not only do we have in both characters the child as seer, we have also a kind of formal initiation into the world of human bedevilment and into the grossness of which people are capable. This evil is more apocalyptic in the case of Huck, who witnesses the brutal shooting of Boggs, the clan butchery of the Grangerford family, and the almost successful attempts of the King and the Duke to steal the patrimony of the Wilks sisters. Still, Sid Tussie views the murder of Uncle Mott and the ingratitude of the Tussies, and he comes to an understanding of the sizable amount of original sin exuding from those Tussies who bilk Grandpa Tussie. Despite the striking parallelism between the two characters, there is probably no conscious influence at work here. Sid's paternity as a literary character goes back at least to G. W. Harris' Sut Lovingood, who was one of the first alienated, déclassé youngsters in American literature. Huck Finn continues the type as, in a modified sense, do Sherwood Anderson's boy protagonists in "I Want to Know Why" and "I'm A Fool."

There are differences, of course; *Huckleberry Finn* ends in a long episode of Tom Sawyer joviality while *Taps* ends in a flutter of violence. *Huckleberry Finn* grew by fits and starts over a ten-year period; *Taps For Private Tussie* was tossed off in six weeks of steady writing. Probably there has been no conscious influence of Twain on Stuart, for both writers had somewhat similar folk backgrounds in their lives and created narrative personae who reflected these similarities. Stuart, of course, vastly admires Twain and in some unconscious way must be influenced by him, since writers as diverse as Hemingway and Faulkner have shown this influence.[5]

Second only to the Huck Finn element in giving charm to the book is the character of Grandpa Tussie. Sid is the method of narration, but Grandpa Tussie is the focus of character. The whole book wheels about Grandpa Tussie, who is the head of the "relief Tussies." He is on stage almost all the time; and, if he disappears for a moment, the reader begins to feel like Sid Tussie, who grows lonesome whenever separated from Grandpa. Grandpa starts the book as a character who is always verging on pure farce and ends close to pathos. This shift in emphasis does not seem consciously designed by Stuart. As the novel moved forward, Stuart became more and more attached to Grandpa and deepened his character and his essential kindness. He becomes, therefore, one of Stuart's most successful characterizations.

Grandpa, at the beginning of the novel, is a spry, seventy year old mountaineer with a white beard stained with ambeer (tobacco spittle), a wild laugh, and an inherited dread of work. Armed with an old age pension check and with government relief, Grandpa can and does defy with impunity all the importunate employers who want him to work in the fields, on the roads, or in the forests. He has emerged as the patriarch, the leader of the "relief Tussies" who vote for the Democrats in order to get on the relief roles even though they are Republican by conviction and history. His conscience, in the form of Grandma Tussie, goads him again and again about selling out his party while the Uncle George Tussies (the non-relief Tussies) have stuck by it. "I've learned to look after number one first," Grandpa said. "Look where we are today. Look where Brother George is!" (p. 81).

Grandpa emerges as a version of the shrewd natural man, a kind of seer who is wiser than he looks and who is the instrument of satire on statist tendencies in modern society. A glorious parasite living off the labor of others, he rejoices in his state except for the fact that he has to walk seven miles to get his relief food. "It's a fur piece to walk after your grub," Grandpa said. "If a man votes for it, b-gad, they ought to deliver it to his door" (p. 40). The farmers working hard in their tobacco field look with mean eyes at the free-loading Tussies passing on the road. The farmers offer money to get the Tussies to work in their tobacco fields, but Grandpa refuses with a wild laugh: "I told 'em I wasn't going to lose what I's a-gettin'. Told 'em I's too old to work and was pensioned" (p. 41). Since relief is the blood of life to Grandpa, one of the major tragedies of his life comes when he is taken off relief for owning property. Sid sympathizes with him: "I knew that it hurt Grandpa to take his relief away from him. He had had it many years; it was something that seemed to him would go on forever and forever. Now it was gone and that was the only thing I had ever seen that had stopped him from dancin' when a dance was a-goin' on to fast and furious music upstairs" (p. 132).

This inherited indolence seems to be the dominant streak in Grandpa, as in all of the "relief Tussies." They all fear work; and, when Uncle Mott says, "But a Tussie can stand anything when he has to," Grandma Tussie answers, "He can stand anything before he'll work to make it better" (p. 168). But Grandpa is more than just an indolent buffoon. Like Jeeter Lester of Erskine Caldwell's *Tobacco Road,* he still holds within him a deep love of the land. After Vittie buys him a fifty-acre farm, Grandpa lifts a handful of leaf-rot loam, lets it run caressingly through his fingers, and says, "It's wonderful to know that this land is mine . . . It's the first time in my life I've ever had a deed for land. This land is mine . . . I'm a proud man to own land" (p. 182). Even as Grandpa lies on his death bed numbering his last few hours, he thinks primarily of the smell of new ground loam in the spring and of the rich crops of corn, beans, and pumpkins that he and Sid could have raised. But he had never owned land before; and, when he does, it is too late.

Sid's deep love of Grandpa is another element countering the buffoon in Grandpa. After all Sid is our focus of narration, and we see all the characters through his eyes, his valuation is the one we accept. Sid leave us in no doubt as to how he stands about Grandpa: "I loved Grandpa more than anybody I had ever known—and when he went away for even a day I wanted to go with him" (p. 148). Sid gets homesick to see Grandpa whenever the old fellow is away: "Grandpa had always taken me with 'im, and I loved 'im. And it was hard for me to stay away from 'im . . . I thought Grandpa was the best man in the world. He'd been the best man to me I had ever known" (p. 214). As Sid divulges more clearly to the reader his intense love for the old man, the transition from pure farce to mingled farce and pathos becomes more obvious; and, by the time Grandpa lies on his deathbed in the closing scenes of the book, we are ready to accept at face value Sid's statement—"Grandpa never cared whether he had anything or not and when he did have something everybody was welcome to it. I'd never seen another man like Grandpa. . . . I know that if he was a-dyin and it took all the grub he had to save him and that if somebody was hungry and asked him for part of it he'd give 'im half of it" (p. 263).

So in his own way Grandpa becomes as central to *Taps For Private Tussie* as Anse Bushman is to *Trees of Heaven;* and, like Anse, he has his own private savor, a delightful one. Perhaps the scene that best conveys this savor is the one in which Grandpa—who lived first under a rock cliff, then in a one-room school house, later in the fine Rayburn house, and is now back in a two-room shack with junk dishes and makeshift furniture—looks happily about him at the bedraggled shack:

> "And we can drink our coffee from teacups and saucers agin," Uncle George said.
>
> "It's more like livin'," Aunt Vittie said.
>
> "I'm a-livin' just the way I like to live," Grandpa said. (p. 196)

And this statement expresses the patriarch's primary quality—he is living *just the way he likes to live.*

At this point, we might ask if this seemingly ingenuous novel displays any thematic complexity. The answer would be—more than one would think at first reading. If we itemize some of the themes that emerge from the whole story, the most obvious is perhaps the running satire on the abuses of government relief. The Tussies are perfectly capable of working, and there are many farmers who offer them jobs, but Grandpa's ready answer to this is—"'I don't haf to work, Grandpa said, 'long as the government feeds me. Why should I work!'" (p. 35). Sid stands in line at the big relief office ("It's one industry that keeps a-growin' right through good times!") and looks at the powerful Tussie men who crowd in to free-load rather than do the work which they are competent to do. "I saw young strong men with big arms and bull necks. I saw Mort, Enic, Thad, Fiddis, Cy, Bolivar, Add, Wade, Sebie, Sid, Bert, and Mule Tussie in the crowd. They were powerful men. I'd seen them carry Uncle Kim in his big black coffin to the top of the mountain where they had dug his grave through the rocks on the mountain top" (p. 51).

So the statist society intrudes into a dying mountain culture and pays for a kind of parasitism which results in the ridiculous spectacle of forty-six bull-necked Tussies crowded into the Rayburn house free-loading on government groceries and drinking Toodle Powell's bootleg booze paid for with Kim's insurance money. They loll about in the yard and finally get too lazy to carry relief grub from town, so Dee and Ben Tussie turn Grandpa in to government authorities to escape carrying any more relief grub. Quotations already used in the discussion of Sid and Grandpa indicate how ubiquitous this satire of big government is throughout the novel. Even Grandpa, the kingpin of the "relief Tussies," turns against the hand that has fed him when he finally lies on his deathbed: " 'When you raise your own corn, beans, taters and pumpkins, you don't haf to depend on relief,' Grandpa said. 'You don't haf to wonder and worry about how long you are a-goin' to hold your relief and about somebody a-reportin' you. And you can vote the way you please. . . . You don't get but seven dollars if you don't vote right. Farmin' is the only sure way' " (p. 271). Grandpa's tragedy is that he was a reliefer too long—he found the truth too late.

Already developed as a theme is Sid's initiation into the world and into the evil in it. Interwoven with this initiation theme is a kind of dream motif: Sid's constant feeling that the great changes his life is undergoing may be dream and not reality. This dream status of his life appears early in the novel when Sid hears Uncle Mott say, "It seems like a dream to me that we're a-goin to move into a mansion and be somebody!" (p. 65). When they finally move into the new house, Sid is overcome on the first night with its splendor and with the transition from the school-room squalor to the immaculate rooms. He lies sleepless in bed: "I wondered if it was a dream that I was dreamin' or if it had happened" (p. 74). He awakes the next morning and feels he's someone else until he looks in the looking glass: "I was the same Sid Tussie

that had lived in the school house. I was just in a different shell"
(p. 78). When Uncle Kim marvelously reappears late in the
novel amid a series of catastrophic events, Sid stands rigid for a
moment with trauma: "And then I thought that it must be a
dream. . . . But I touched one kitchen wall with my hand and
the wall had a strange feelin'. . . . It wasn't a dream, for I was
awake with my people in a world where we lived, breathed and
died" (p. 294).

Midnight approaches. "Uncle Mott was dead, Grandpa was
dyin' and Uncle Kim was livin', all in the same room. It all
seemed so much like a dream to me and made thoughts go
through my head and fade like morning mists. . . . It seemed
like a dream, but it wasn't a dream for I felt life surge through
my body and I felt warmth from the big fire" (p. 303). Undoubtedly the word "fire" bears a latent symbolic meaning relating it to the fire of life. And Sid's constant feeling that life is
inseparable from dream is one he shares with Mark Twain, who
held the same conviction and affirmed it to be the highest wisdom
in his novelette, *The Mysterious Stranger*.

Among other themes, there is that of the pleasure of human
togetherness. As noted earlier in this chapter, Stuart was fascinated by the idea of people banding together to eat, sing, and
just be together. The Tussie family, including Vittie and Sid,
move as a unit from cliff to school house to mansion to shack.
There are no "loners" in the family; they support one another
and contribute to the good of the total family. Uncle George
joins them and is absorbed into this total group. At the Rayburn
house the family swells monstrously to forty-six mouths so they
have to prepare three tables and have a second sitting for two
of them. This communal joy of togetherness reaches its climax
in the great dances held each night by the Tussie clan in the
ballroom of the Rayburn house. Indolent and shiftless as they
are, this dancing is sufficient justification for their way of life.
Sid describes these dances: "I've never seen anything like the
dances we had, as many as four sets a-dancin' at the time. Watt
Tussie was a guitar picker, Sebie played the jews-harp and Dave
Tussie played the french-harp. Many nights we danced all night.
Life went on in the George Rayburn house as it had never gone
before. All we did was eat, dance, and be merry. And there was
plenty of lovin a-goin on" (p. 124).

To turn for a moment from the substance of the book to its

general form, we can say that the themes mentioned above exist organically in a style marked by the hyperbole of frontier humor, by irony and satire, and by a clear idiom mildly flavored with dialect. Many of the scenes and quotations already used in this discussion are evidence of this frontier humor and of the satire on the relief practices of the omnicompetent state. Occasionally an ironic touch appears. Uncle Mott, for instance, returns home after killing Ben and Dee Tussie; and he incongruously comes bearing a box of chocolates for Vittie in his blood-stained hands— a love offering which he places on his bed. In a few minutes Mott is dead, shot through the head by Uncle George; and Kim comes in and lifts Mott's dead body, "carried him to Uncle Mott's old bed, laid him on it beside the box of candy he had brought for Aunt Vittie, and covered him with a sheet" (p. 294). So Vittie receives a double gift—candy and a corpse.

Stuart's style is not heavily symbolic, but the symbols used take off from a good concrete physical image and are readily comprehensible. One of the best is the spider-fly image used to foreshadow Grandpa's death. Grandpa gets a token of his approaching death and lies in his bed watching a fly caught in a spider's web on the ceiling above him. He watches the spider eat the fly while he tells Sid how well he would have farmed had he lived. But Grandpa grows weaker even as he talks, for Grandpa is the fly and Time the spider that had sapped the life from him. He talks on, growing weaker and weaker, and Sid realizes what is happening: "There was no use for 'im to talk about beans, taters, pumpkins, and corn now. The spider had eaten the fly" (p. 272).

Thus the symbols are firmly grounded in images. The whole narrative, in fact, is remarkable for the solid imagery which anchors it firmly to actuality. Homely folk figures of speech fall naturally into the dialogue, as when Vittie protests too strongly that her heart lies in a mountain grave with Kim and that she had no intent of getting married again. " 'But a woman's comb gets red again,' Grandpa said, 'when she is still young and pretty and don't have her a man!' " (p. 37). Occasional dialect words show up: "They [Grandpa and Uncle Mott] had a good time a-goin' places together until they got tanked on rotgut and fursed with one another" (p. 41). "Fursed" for "fussed" is a mountain expression and is used several times in *Taps*. Other dialect expressions are: "cornswaggled," "pliam-blank," "a-doddlin'," and "given up to be." Grandpa also has a store of folk aphorisms which he uses on appropriate occasions, as when he warns Mott not to antagonize Uncle George and Vittie because they hold the whip hand, cautioning, "When you get your hand in a bear's mouth. . . . you'd better work easy till you get it out" (p. 252).

The book's ending has bothered some critics, who feel that the novel just wanders around following the antics of the Tussie clan until Stuart grows weary and miraculously brings Kim to life again. But the ending is not so inconclusive as they imply; it serves as a kind of cathartic effect for the reader. All through the story Sid has been wondering *how* Kim would feel if he could see all the goings on of the Tussie clan; there is strong foreshadowing here and the reader feels as strongly as Sid about this reaction. How would the dead warrior feel if he could return and find his brother and uncle taking his wife, the whole greedy clan eating and drinking up his insurance money, society laying waste the country for which he was fighting—himself and his country forgotten? The resurrection of Private Kim Tussie from the dead provides answers to some of these questions and relief to the reader. It dramatizes succinctly the picture of parasites (Grandpa Tussie and family) supporting other parasites (the "Relief Tussies"). Grandpa's dying soliloquy makes clear that for Stuart the "Relief Tussies" really represent Everyman in the Welfare State. It reaffirms the primacy of the themes of love in Sid's love of Grandpa and Stuart's ever-recurring note of optimism and vitalism in Sid's affirmation of life in the last sentence of the novel. The ending says that while one leader has gone, Kim has replaced him and life will surge through Kim and Sid into future and unforseeable forms.

Regarded in these terms, *Taps For Private Tussie* is no inconsiderable novel. On the surface, Stuart seems like a painter of primitive art—he gives big, strong scenes and does so in big, strong colors. There seems no concern for subtlety as such; but, in retrospect, as this discussion has attempted to point out, there are nuances of meaning which intrigue the imagination of the reader. In one respect a boisterous ballad of lolling reliefers and inherited indolence, the novel is, in a lesser key, a sad-comic pastorale of a family caught in the turbulence of acute social change and not realizing the why of all the turbulence. The popularity of the work should not blind us to the fact that it possesses genuine narrative merit and that real exuberance which is so much a hallmark of Jesse Stuart. Stuart's intuition for trends is marvelously exhibited here. When we read the newspaper today, we suddenly realize that the Tussies are no longer confined to the Kentucky mountains—the "relief Tussies" are all around us. But Stuart is an artist, not a polemicist. He does not inveigh against the welfare state—he laughs with Press Tussie who says, "I'm a-livin' just the way I like to live." Press Tussie is tolerant, and so is Jesse Stuart.

IV   Foretaste of Glory

One of the advantages of writing about a living author is that he is still around to answer questions about the genesis of his various works. Stuart remembers that *Foretaste of Glory* began, as it were, by accident. During his service in the navy in World War II he began one day to tell stories about home-town characters to fellow officers in his writing unit. When his commander told him to write them up, he did, working a solid two months, utilizing leave time, Sundays, nights, and every spare moment he could. The wartime rush was on, and he completed the last details of the manuscript with his publisher in New York City over the phone from Washington, D.C.

The book was published in 1946 and, Stuart says, "When I went home the reaction against me in the home town over this book was terrible."[6] In fact, Stuart thought at one time that he would leave Greenup County to avoid the acrimony. Greenup reacted, then, very much as Asheville, North Carolina, did when Thomas Wolfe exposed a cross section of it in *Look Homeward, Angel.* Wolfe was threatened with mayhem and a public lynching if he returned; he stayed away seven years and returned to enormous public acclaim, all threats forgotten. Stuart, however, returned to face the public acerbity and, as we have noted, had the satisfaction of seeing a statue erected in his honor in front of the court house at Greenup in 1955.

This account of the beginning of *Fortaste of Glory* leads us into its essential character and structure. The structure, which gives the novel its character, consists of a series of short stories occurring at the same place and time but having, for the most part, different characters. The place is Blakesburg; the time the night of September 18, 1941. The characters are all residents of

Blakesburg whose lives are brought to a climax or an anticlimax by the apocalyptic appearance of the aurora borealis, never before seen by them and taken to be a portent of the second coming of Christ and of the end of the world. Each chapter or episode is self-contained and concentrates on telling the life story of one individual and of showing how he or she reacts to the final summons (as each believes it to be).

In one sense, reading this novel is like pacing through a hall of echoes. As the reader proceeds from chapter to chapter, he is reminded of a number of other novels, or poems with novelized forms, that employ structures so similar and in some senses so bizarre that the reader becomes unduly conscious of the structural element. Vicki Baum's *Grand Hotel* lays great emphasis on time and place, as does Stuart's novel. Anderson's *Winesburg, Ohio* tells a series of short stories, all of which occur in one town; *Foretaste* is much like this except that Stuart's tone is lightly ironic without any of Anderson's throat-clutching style.

Stuart employs a kind of choral authorial voice which points out the foibles and ironies flashing before us on the stage. We can see an analogy to Masters' *Spoon River Anthology*, with both narratives dramatizing the moment of truth, the subterranean reality running under what the public sees, as in the case of Judge Allie Anderson, long a pillar of civic pride and integrity, who confesses to being the father of the illegitimate boy, Rufus Litteral, and to concealing and lying about it for seventeen years in order to protect himself and to ruin his political enemies. But Stuart differs in tone; he unveils Blakesburg's hypocrites without the harshness of Masters toward those of *Spoon River*.

While dealing with the poetry analogy, we could point out that *Foretaste* bears a discernible resemblance to Stuart's own *Man with a bull-tongue Plow*, which tells in poetry a series of condensed short stories all occurring in the same place. The difference again is that the tone of the poetry volume is not only more lyric, but harsher and more heavily ironic than *Foretaste*. Other echoes come to the reader—we note in passing Katherine Anne Porter's *Ship of Fools*, where the place image is a ship, and Thornton Wilder's *Bridge of San Luis Rey*, where the place image is diminished even more to an Indian bridge. So Stuart has adopted a device employed usually as a virtuoso technique, or a tour de force, and well known though not too frequently used (Glenway Wescott in *The Grandmothers* uses the device of a family album to impose a kind of place unity on his narrative).

The structure, then, is highly episodic; and the action of the first episode begins in the wild, helter-skelter flight of Liam Winston, who comes shooting through the dining room of Aunt Effie Winston's boarding house at breakneck speed. Judge Whittlecomb jumps up from his game of solitaire: "What's the matter, Liam?" "'The goddamned world's a-comin to a end, Judge,' he panted, making for the door that opened onto Main Street."[7] When Liam goes panting out into the street to find his estranged brother, Booten, a flashback gives us an account of a murderous but hilarious fight between the two brothers. Liam finds Booten and begs him to forgive before time ends:

> "No never," Booten roared. . . . "I know the end of time has come but I don't give a damn. . . . Thar'll be a lot a-going to hell with me. And the devil will know that I've been a fair fighter! . . . But by-god he'll be afraid o' you! Ye'll be lookin' fer a soft place to stick yer knife in his back. . . . And ye know damned well Jesus Christ won't have ye! . . . I don't know what the hell's a-goin' to happen to ye, Liam!" (p. 18)

Booten plunges across the street to hear "Old Glory" Gardner give his last talk on Blakesburg and the flag. Liam stands with cooking spatula in hand, garbed in his dirty grease-stained apron, his teeth rattling in fear.

This good, exuberant opening scene, with a kind of wild John Skelton humor in it, creates a tempo and a comic extravagance that not all of the succeeding episodes can maintain. But it sets a tone which is essentially right for the whole work. This tone, so integral to the success of the book, is satiric; but its intent has almost no connection with that of the Sinclair Lewis of *Main Street* and *Babbitt*. Rather it is a throwback to the old Southwestern humor of Jonce Hooper, A. B. Longstreet, and G. W. Harris. Like them, Stuart's spirit is that of anecdotal whimsy, showing us human foibles for the sake of laughter. It is a kind of pure narrative swimming up from an older, agrarian America, free of any real animus toward the creatures described. He *likes* Liam Winston, who is convinced that the "goddamned world's coming to an end, Judge!"; and "Old Glory" Gardner, the flag maniac; and Muff Henderson, the "dancerholic" who has two-stepped three wives to exhaustion and is about to crack up a fourth; and Mary Blanton, who has a stable of male lovers. The choral voice of the old-time raconteur, which comes through strong and clear, bears few philosophical overtones; but human comedy is implicit in some of these portraits.

There are, for instance, Pat Greenough and Aliss Dinwiddy, the last leaves on two rival family trees; they go with each other for years but never marry. When the *"Lights!"* hit them, they course through town hand-in-hand to a secluded spot on the river bank; there, a village *voyeur* discovers them enjoying a last carnal coupling before going to glory. There is also Tid Fortner, Blakesburg's well-dressed and abstemious king bootlegger who, though a bachelor, keeps a large supply of divorced women and unwed mothers in his home to the scandalous relish of the town. The *"Lights!"* send him racing across town toward his private harem.

Malinda Sprouse, Amazonian laundress and money lender and now the richest person in town, hurries around collecting all the laundry and interest debts owed her; she figures that, if this is the end of the world, she'll take it with her. Aged aristocrat Nellie Blake, who lives in a converted stable after having had one home burned and one ruined by the flood, answers Malinda's warning of apocalypse by saying, "I've moved from a flood; I've been burned out by a fire, and I'm not moving again. Let the world end" (p. 101). And there are the prisoners in the county jail, freed in the height of the *"Lights"* hysteria who come trooping out, take one look at the apocalyptic sky, and moan, "Hits a hell of a poor time to free us now" (p. 210).

This exuberant satiric tone is not, however, the only unifying factor; for, as the reader moves along, he discovers that certain motifs recur in stories throughout the novel (or so we will call it, for want of a better term). The thematic motifs that help bind the narrative together include the rise of the Red Necks. We soon learn that the town of Blakesburg is dominated by two old families, the Greenoughs and the Dinwiddies, who are the aristocrats of the town and who belong to rival political parties and churches. The equivalent of Faulkner's Sartorises, Compsons, and DeSpains, they represent culture and gentility; but their culture and gentility are going to seed. Pat Greenough, last of his family, sells his old home, keeps a few family heirlooms and rents a room in a boarding house, not deigning to work. Miss Aliss, last of her family, loses her money, lives alone in her old home, and with the passing of the years gradually fades back into the wallpaper. While the blueblood Greenoughs and Din-widdies ran to seed, the new life was being brought to town by the Red Necks: the crude country cousins from the hills beyond Blakesburg.

When the ancient Greenough party seems about dead, a Red Neck, Judge Allie Anderson, revivifies it. The Judge maintains his political hegemony by an unbeatable stratagem—he keeps a pigpen at his home just a block off Main Street. Here the people from the hills who elected Judge Allie could come at eventide when he slopped his hogs; they talked of farming, feeling at home as they never could in his plush office in the courthouse, and asked their little favors of him. The more the town people complained of the stench of the pig sty just a block off the court square, the more votes Judge Allie got from the hill people. This made Judge Allie "just a common man" to Black County voters. Judge Allie was not only part of the "Rise of the Red Necks," he was their champion.

Muff Henderson, who took to dancing as some men take to drink and drugs, wears out three wives who try to two-step from night to morning with him. Muff, who looks for a year for a fourth wife, one day discovers a young Red Neck girl, Doshie Kegley, plowing a tobacco patch. She had strong muscular arms and legs, and enough wind to run down a pig that had gotten out of the pen. Recognizing that Doshie is built for a dancer, he marries her: "and she's stayed with me six years! Doshie's a powerful dancer if ever I danced with one!" (p. 57). The Red Neck blood triumphed again.

No one looked with greater scorn on the rise of the Red Necks than Willie Deavers, who was born of highly respected "Blue Blood" stock on both sides of the house. Willie prophesied that the Red Necks would eventually get control of all the business, political offices, and churches in Blakesburg and in Blake County. He also forecast that the old families would be swallowed by these hard-working, hard-fighting, heavy-drinking, fanatically praying Red Necks. "Blue-Blood" Willie, who never worked, dallied and read his life away on the inheritance his parents had left him. But Willie finally meets and marries beautiful Sylvia Moore, daughter of a well-known Red Neck family; and he eventually succumbs to work, thus furthering the Red Neck rise to hegemony in town and county.

Stuart is manipulating his own little comic myth with the Blue Bloods, decadent and lethargic, and the Red Necks, boisterous, crude, and sometimes beautiful. To return for a moment to the Faulknerian analogy, if the Blue Bloods are equivalent to Faulkner's Compsons and Sartorises, then the Red Necks are similar to Faulkner's Snopeses. They share with the Snopes clan a lack of family position and breeding, a country crudity, and a rural background; they share also a fertility and ubiquity which makes them seem to spring up everywhere and to be taking over everything; like the Snopeses, they are opportunistic and quick to get ahead. Unlike the Snopeses, however, they are neither villainous nor parasitic. There are no Red Necks who compare with the heartlessness of Flem Snopes and his predatory kinsmen. But, if the tone is different, the reality is just as great. There were some real Snopeses taking over Faulkner's Oxford, and there are real Red Necks taking over Greenup. In fact, quite a number were out for Stuart's head after *Foretaste* was published. But they were needlessly alarmed, for a close scrutiny shows that Stuart's heart was with them all through the book. Although on the Red Neck side, he cannot help laughing at them; but his laughter does not hurt the novel.

The theme commented on by most reviewers of *Foretaste* is hypocrisy. Some have seen the novel as primarily a jab at the moral hypocrites who pretend to be paragons of virtue. The gallery of hypocrites in *Foretaste* includes Judge Allie Anderson, father of fourteen children, devoted to his wife, and called by all the county "a good old-fashioned family man." The very image of rural probity until the "*Lights!*" flared up, Judge Allie, filled with a vision of the last judgment, goes to the hut of the lonely Rufus Litteral, seventeen years old, an orphaned and illegitimate child without any knowledge of who his real father was. Rufus, ostracized by the town, lives in need of human companionship. When the Judge comes at the last gasp of time, he confesses to being his father and to having set afloat rumors charging other men with being the father of Rufus because they would "help me politically" (p. 37). But Rufus is not ready to forgive his hypocrite father: "I'm not proud of you, Pappie." And in the end Rufus rejects the father who has so long rejected him; he wants nothing to do with a father who has been so late in coming to his aid.

Hypocrite number two is Attorney Joe Oliver, mighty lawyer and scourge of sinners and criminals:

> . . . the good people in the town thought Joe one of their most prominent citizens. They knew he wouldn't take a divorce case unless it was one of immoral charges against the husband or wife. People knew that Joe was a "clean, decent and upright gentleman of great moral integrity." He had taught most of the town's young people in his famous Sunday School Class. (p. 38)

When the "*Lights!*" come, this paragon of excellence lies writhing on the bed, sweating like the helpless witness he has vilified in court; he slowly confesses that the housemaid, Red Neck Mattie Pratt, has been his mistress for fifteen years. When morning comes, Mrs. Joe Oliver is seen climbing the steps to Attorney Jason Broughton's office—Blakesburg's successful divorce lawyer.

Other portraits in Blakeburg's gallery of hypocrites include Alex Scroggins, the county attorney who prosecutes the liquor dealers of the town and boasts in court of the clean and wholesome life he leads personally; in actuality, he drives his car each evening to a hiding place in the country where he tipples in secret. Then there is Poodi Troxler, undertaking genius and top assistant of Marvin Clayton, who gets all of the undertaking business of the Greenough clan. Poodi is upright and gregarious, a friend to both Greenough and Dinwiddie regardless of party. He even makes frequent friendly visits to the undertaking establishment of Marvin Clayton's great rival, Franklin Foster. But the "*Lights!*" come, Poodi and wife embrace for the last time, and Poodi has a confession to make to her: "I've been a-stealin' tools from Franklin Foster!" (p. 136). Last of the hypocrites is white-haired Charley Albright, one of the courtyard philosophers, who has a disability clause in his insurance contract, became crippled after a short illness, and gets around on crutches. Come the "*Lights!*" and the end of the world, and crippled Charlie throws away his crutches and takes off down the street like a frightened quail leaving a cane brake. " 'If the world don't end, Charlie's shore as God lost his insurance this time,' Booten Winston said to Boliver Tussie as Charlie passed by them like a shot out of a gun" (p. 242).

There is a question as to whether or not the Reverend Perry Rhoden would be called a hypocrite; Reverend Rhoden's family is indigent indeed until he decides to cut in on the "quickie wedding" business, which is so profitable financially to the justice of the peace and to the other ministers of the town. He prays over his decision and gets the approval of the Lord; but as a salve to his conscience, he gives twenty-five per cent of his profits to the Lord for a new church. The money rolls in, and the Rhoden family lives in fine fettle. The Reverend Rhoden is marrying a couple when suddenly the "*Lights!*" appear. The Reverend drops to his knees and prays to God, promising *all* of his money to the new church if God will but stay "His Hand of Destruction."

Other examples of hypocrisy can be dredged from the book, but to speak of the novel as an anatomy of hypocrisy, as some critics have done, is surely to miss the humor with which Stuart contemplated, and evidently meant for his readers to contemplate, his gallery of hypocrites. On the night of September 18, when the "*Lights!*" hit Greenup, Kentucky, Stuart himself was out all night soaking up the Skeltonian saturnalia. He enjoyed it in real life, and he lets this enjoyment soak through to his fiction. Stuart reminds us that in the house of fiction, there is room for two kinds of satire: his and Masters'.

Evangelical Protestantism permeates Blakesburg, and many of the episodes treat some phase of this influence. Greenup natives objected to Stuart's portrayal of religion. As his general attitudes toward religion are indicated in the episodes, one of the most obvious is his view of confession. When the heavens open and declare the coming of Judgment Day, sinful man is impelled to confess. These penitents make their confessions without authorial comment from Stuart. We meet, as we have already noted, all sorts of penitent sinners, such as Bass Kenton, horse trader and alcoholic, who sees the burning skies and knows that the savior is coming: "And I'm not ready to meet him. . . . He won't have any use for me, a hoss swapper and a sot" (p. 155). In the episode of Noah Billups, Stuart mingles folklore and religion. Noah was the meanest man in town and the biggest drunk, and people said he and his wife had signed a pact with the devil. Old Jinnie Slemp, the midwife, said that Noah's fourth child was devil-marked and that Noah buried it at night far up on the mountains. Boys tried to dig up the devil's child, but the devil sent thunder, lightning, and rain to drive them away. Noah and his wife dress their children in white, ready to go up to the golden throne—all, that is, except their boy Herbie, who is told that his dog, Bob, can't go with him because there are no dogs in heaven. " 'But I don't wanta go,' Herbie wailed. 'I don't want to without old Bob!' " (p. 161).

Stuart's most obvious comment on the Pharisees of this world comes in the episode of Temperance and Ollie Spradling. Temp and Oll get drunk together and at a certain stage of drunkenness are impelled to go into the middle of Main Street, where Temp systematically batters her husband into unconsciousness, a ritual which Oll takes as an expression of her love. Temp has just showed her love for the hundredth time by putting Ollie down for the count when the *"Lights!"* appear; then Temp, looking up in fear, faints dead away. Her pulse is weak, and Sam Porter is afraid she's going to die; he approaches Flossie Herald:

> "Ain't you a Christian?" Sam asked. . . .
> "I'm a Christian but I won't have nothing to do with 'er," Flossie said. . . .
> "That sinful old trollop," Bertie Caldwell said as she ran past Temp lying in the street.
> Bertie Caldwell was a worker in one of the best churches in Blakesburg.
> "Leave 'er be," Roy Oliver said to Damon Thombs, both deacons in a church, as they hurried by. (pp. 204-5)

The Blakesburg Pharisees hasten by unheeding, so Sam Porter has to call on two of the town's most prominent publicans, Boliver Tussie, notorious Red Neck drunk, and Tid Fortner, king of the bootleggers. Tussie and Fortner help carry Temp to the docter's office, and there the biblical contrast between the Pharisees and the publicans is clearly made in a kind of modern morality.

Stuart gives the final episode to a religious contrast. The Reverend Whitstone, a sane and quiet retired minister who recognizes the *"Lights!"* as merely an aurora borealis and tries to tell the people, is denounced on all sides. Bert Edgewater, an excitable exhorter from one of the Holiness churches, denounces the Reverend Whitstone for his unfaithfulness and begins to circle the court house, praising God at the top of his voice. Sister Spence, a buxom exhorter and preacher, stands in the courtyard with penitent sinners writhing at her feet and with guitars and hymn singing adding to the general alarm about her. When she preaches about a God of wrath, Reverend Whitstone reminds her that God is love. But her exhorters denounce him and threaten him with violence, making him move on to his home. He walks slowly homeward, saying: "It's strange but when you tell people the truth, they won't believe you" (p. 253).

Really, then, the judicious reader cannot find much to fault Stuart in his portrayal of religion in Blakesburg. Blakesburg, as he portrays it, displays a religious spectrum pretty much like that of a thousand other small American communities. Blakesburg has its quota of hypocrites, fanatics, and Pharisees; but it also has Rufus Litteral and Reverend Whitstone whom we can admire in the exercise of their religious probity. So Stuart is not attacking religion; rather, it is one element in a vast, panoramic scene, à la Peter Breughel's peasant canvases; Stuart delights in the complexity of the scene and is fascinated by human foibles as well as by human heroism.

Counterpointing the religious motif in *Foretaste* is what might be called the liquor motif, and this motif seems the more important of the two to the natives of Blakesburg. What would Blakesburg be without whisky? Intolerably dull, if we judge from corn and sugar whisky which flows in a great, vitalizing wave through Blakesburg. This wave flows into the thirsty gullets of Liam Winston; of Temp and Oll Spradling, the pugilistic lovers; of Uncle Jeff Hargis, who lolls drunkenly in a cow stall with two gallon jugs of sugar whisky by his side and straws to drink from the jugs when he is too drunk to lift his head; of Dee Addington, the town pretty boy and Don Juan; of Bill Simpson, failed boxer but successful restaurateur and bootlegger; of Horsefly Salyers, who uses the imagined infidelities of his loyal wife as his excuse for boozing. Whisky is really the "water of life"—the social lubricant which keeps Blakesburg's communal life smoothly articulating. "Licker" is the key to a hundred comic situations in *Foretaste*.

In the epilogue, which bears the title, "The Next Morning," we see Blakesburg gradually adjust to continued life after a night of Apocalypse. A sluggish current of life oozes across the square, jazzed up a bit by the sweet solace of "licker." "Just as soon as Bill Haddington unlocked his Beer Parlor, they watched Liam Winston who was shaky as a leaf in the winter wind, shoot ahead of Bill through the door like a bullet!" (p. 255). Liam emerges a few minutes later without "the shakes" and methodically wiping his lips. He has a gleam in his eye as he walks steadily up the street past the Citizen's Bank toward the Winston Boarding House. Liam is symbolic of Everyman in Blakesburg. All over Blakesburg citizens are bracing themselves for the day with a swig of pure corn if they're well-to-do or of sugar whisky if they're in the lower brackets. All over Blakesburg nervous citizens are preparing to head for town, knowing Blakesburg will endure as long as Tid Fortner still purveys his matchless corn liquor. "Old Reliable Tid," as they called him, was still at his post. Blakesburg and the Republic still stood. *Aqua vitae vincit omnia.*

Looking back over what has been said about *Foretaste,* we feel that the novel was not justly adjudged by book reviewers and critics. Its essence was missed. Full of exuberant life and fun, *Foretaste* is really quite close to being a literary analogue to a Bruegel the Elder painting (such as "Peasant Wedding" or "Peasant Dance" or "Land of Cockaigne"). Like Stuart, Bruegel the Elder was noted for his realistic depictions of village life. His contemporaries called him "Peasant Bruegel" and "The Droll." He was a keen observer of nature and the everyday life of his Flemish environment, displaying in his work a robust and often humorous concern with the daily occupation and foibles of his fellow men.

All the above statements are about equally true of *Foretaste of Glory.* It, too, is about village life, here highlighted by a moment of threatened Apocalypse. In this, as in all his other works, Stuart remains the keenest observer of nature in current American fiction. *Foretaste* is robust and humorous, and it plays good naturedly on the foibles of the native Blakesburgers. Finally, there is a great healthy love and affirmation of life in both Stuart and Bruegel the Elder. After viewing the giant panorama of Blakesburg's comic Apocalypse, painted in thirty-six different panels, we come away with a strong sense of exuberant affirmation of the life force. Life, after all, is good in Blakesburg; and, as the novel plays out its final scene, we see two of the archangels of Blakesburg's court square, Bass Keaton and Uncle Sweeter Dabney, whittling quietly away on a courtyard bench: ". . . life was so good to them. They were sitting on their favorite spot of earth while Old Glory rippled above their beloved Blakesburg and life went on for them and their city like the slow turning of a paddle wheel pushing a steamboat up the broad river" (p. 256).

CHAPTER 5

The Minor Novels

I Mongrel Mettle

IN 1944 Stuart published *Mongrel Mettle*, a novelette[1] about Jerry-B Boneyard, his sister Glenna's dog, that delighted a dual audience of children and adults and bemused critics who didn't quite know how to regard the overtones of social satire which begin to pipe up about midway through the book. The story is a beast fable, a dissertation on mongrelism, a serenade to the poetry of the great dark earth, and a picaresque account of the adventures of a puppy who passes to middle age in the scale of a dog's life.

Stuart picks the ancient life-as-journey motif as the structural principle of his novelette. The story begins with the seven days of darkness that Jerry-B Boneyard knew as a puppy and carries him through five years of adventure, many masters, and a sojourn with foxes, when he goes back to the wild for a winter season. The novelette ends with him secure with his first mistress, Glenna; and the last scene shows Jerry-B trotting beside his pedigreed wife, Dossie, into the sunrise of an August morning. In this sense the story has the simplicity of the ancient archetypal tales which begin in darkness and journey toward the light. Jerry-B's journey is calibrated for us by his name, for he acquires a new and additional name with each master. He begins the tale as Jerry-Boneyard and ends as Jerry-B Boneyard Powderjay Dodderidge Fox Hammonds Lakin Hammertight Blevins Doore, the Mongrel. The acquiring of the name and of new masters gives a rhythm to the story. Jerry-B arrives at a new home, adjusts to it, and lives happily for a while. Then a deep unease falls on him, and one day he shoves off searching for something he has not found. Eventually he comes to a new home, adjusts himself, and lives happily for a while until the same sense of incompletion falls on him, and the cycle begins over again. Thus Jerry-B dramatizes life-as-journey.

Jerry-B starts his journey into the great world because he wants a master to serve when his mistress, Glenna, goes off to college. But, once launched on this journey, he finds that Mort Dodderidge, his first master, is a cruel man; and Jerry-B flees into the woods with his master's buckshot rattling under his skin. When he comes into the cool darkness of the woods, he finds a cave and a couple of foxes who bring him food while he nurses his wounds and crawls slowly back to health.

All through Stuart's work runs a strong love of the wild, the primitive, the great, secret, dark earth. Jerry-B finds that he is not immune to this call of the wild; and, when he recovers from his wounds, he joins the foxes in their secret harryings of the night-bound earth. Jerry-B, who renounces the mastery of man, rejoices in the wild freedom of the foxes:

> Foxes would never be servants for man. They were too much in love with the night, too much in love with the good old wild life that appeals to the nature of dogs; too much in love with the blowing wind at night that carries the scent of rabbits, snowbirds and coveys of quail that think they are hidden in the tall grasses away from the prying noses of the sly ensnaring foxes.[2]

Jerry-B finds that in the dark, funky woods his life now keens with ecstasy. He describes a paradisal run:

> Soon we were lost in the wild desolate woods. It was a happy hunting ground for me. . . . The great dark earth where there wasn't the scent of a human footstep—where the winds moaned overhead—where the dark trees stood bending in the wind and where the blue streams of mountain water ran. This was paradise. This was heaven—to live with the foxes in the great wild woods. Now I was the happiest that I had ever been in my life for I had the freedom that I had always yearned for, a freedom which I had never known. (p. 74)

When Jerry-B finds an Eve in this wild paradise, he thinks about marrying her and living in the forest forever with the foxes—letting his blood go back to something that it once was, something of the wild nature that has come back to him. Fair Fox is the name of the dainty young vixen that he begins to run with. All through the winter they course over the dark mountains, and Jerry-B is happy in this tandem hunt. Then comes late February, and Fair Fox is distracted by foxes barking during the night-time hunt. Jerry-B fears he will lose her; and on a night in March, when many foxes bark at her, he turns from a rabbit hole to give her his catch and finds she has slipped off into the night to rejoin her own clan. She never returns and her defection ends the call of the wild for Jerry-B. Now he feels instead the call of tilled land, a master, soft food. He leaves the foxes and heads toward the valley and a farm house and man.

As Jerry-B bounds down the hill toward civilization, the mood of the book changes; the dark poetry of the earth fades out, and Jerry-B becomes a kind of garrulous canine *picaro* wandering through different strata of mountain society and commenting on the foibles of his various masters. His initial naïveté gives way to a kind of tongue-in-cheek air when he pauses for a while at the home of Master Hollis Hammonds and observes the marital infidelities of Master Hollis and his subsequent abandonment of his wife for pretty Eliza Moltenbright. When Master Hollis sickens and dies, Jerry-B attends the funeral and observes both wives weeping over his dead master. In Jerry's opinion, dog lives never get so mixed up as do those of humans; dog lives are far more sensible. Jerry-B would never have betrayed Fair Fox.

Jerry-B's picaresque journey leads him next to the town of Greenupsburg, where he finds additional scope for his social satire. He finds that soft city life has corrupted all the city dogs, who have sold their canine birthrights for a mess of urban pottage. Max, a big German police dog, corners Jerry and pours out his frustration: "We are in this city a soft generation of dogs going down to something softer and there isn't anything we can do about it. . . . Where is the wild earth? . . . Where is the life that we have known; where, oh where is the earth that we have loved and lost?" (p. 126). Jerry-B then races Max to the top of a hill and beats him badly just to show how soft the city dogs really are.

The hut of a moonshiner is Jerry-B's next stop. His job is to guard the mash barrels; in return, he is allowed to eat all the mash he wants. The mash tastes wonderful but gives him wild dreams each night and leaves him with a hangover when he awakens each morning. But eating it soon gets to be a habit; in short, Jerry-B becomes an alcoholic. He pauses at a spring one day to look at his reflection: "My sad dark eyes looked bloated— . . . My face looked terrible—. . . . fat and full. I looked like a dog that was ready to die" (p. 147). He would like to leave and recover his health, but can't break away from his bondage to sour mash. Doubtless he would have soon declined to a drunkard's grave had not a crew of "Gover-mint" men arrived to chop up the still and the mash barrels and to cart the bootleggers off to the penitentiary, thus relieving him from his bondage to John Barley-corn.

Finally Jerry-B heads back toward the Powderjay farm, where he had been a pup and had grown to young doghood: "In the world of human beings, I had been away five years. In the world of dogs, I had been away half of a lifetime. . . . Now I had seen the world, and was coming back." "Now as I reflected on the seriousness of a dog's life, I thought about Red-Rusty and old Robert" (p. 161). Red-Rusty, the first to greet Jerry-B as he comes in sight of the Powderjay's white farm house, is a pedigreed Irish Setter who comes running out with his "Irish up," barking at Jerry-B. Red-Rusty is an aristocratic New England dog, a Congregationalist and a Republican. Five years ago he had flaunted his pedigree and his long name over Jerry-B's mongrel-ism. Now the two dogs lie down together to exchange notes over the events of the past five years.

Jerry-B soon notes a startling change in Red-Rusty's ideology. Red-Rusty the aristocrat now plumps for democracy and mongrelism in the world of dogs; he has suddenly become a democrat and a liberal. The change had occurred when his master Shan had tried to select a wife for Red-Rusty and had brought a pedigreed Irish Setter and tried to put them in the woodshed together. Red-Rusty balked: "I wouldn't go in the woodshed with her. I showed Master Shan my teeth; I growled furiously; I cursed violent oaths. I think a dog should be allowed to choose his wife—his loved one." (p. 173). When Jerry-B praises him for this change, Red-Rusty begins a political harangue:

> I am getting like you, Jerry-B Boneyard. I've seen the twist and turn of things. I have seen the light. I believe in mongrelism. It is the survival of this country of dogs. . . . we'll be a great nation of dogs. There'll be nothing under the sun like us, but not if we are pedigreed with a stamp and seal and are forced to marry one of our own breed forever. . . . No more pedigreeing for

me! . . . My wife will be a mongrel! I love the mixture of all
dogs in my wife and then our children will get the best there is
in all the races. (p. 174)

Jerry-B, pleased at this change in his former friend, finds that
Trusty-Red-Rusty has improved his vocabulary and that he now
uses powerful words, "such as proletariat, revolution, counter-
revolution, the internationale. . . . I had always been a liberal
dog, but he was going farther with his views than I could go"
(p. 176). Still, Jerry-B feels reassured by Red-Rusty's change of
attitude and political alignment and decides to stay with him:
"I would share Trusty-Red-Rusty's bones for the future—since
Trusty-Red-Rusty had changed his creed and become a liberal."
When ". . . Shan threw bread and bones to us; . . . I knew old
democratic Trusty-Red-Rusty would share with me" (pp. 184-5).
But the bread and bones ended the friendship; for, as soon as
Red-Rusty sees Jerry-B eating the bread and bones, he leaps
viciously at him and scuffs Jerry-B's neck with his teeth: There'll
be no sharing of food. Jerry-B retreats growling and tells the
Irish Setter that he is not a democratic dog, that he is only a
make-believe democratic dog dressed in fine sheep's clothing.
Later Jerry-B, speaking to his beautiful mate Dossie, sums up
his opinion of his former friend: " 'Trusty-Red-Rusty is a Radi-
cal. . . . He talks one way and acts another. He believes in
sharing bones and bread until he has to share it with a pal. . . .
He is a bad dog" (pp. 199-200).

Mingled with this satire on well-to-do aristocrats becoming
liberals and radicals and sharing wealth so long as it isn't theirs
is the theme of Jerry-B's mongrelism, the longest sustained one
in the book. Jerry-B remembers that he was still a pup when his
mother told him that he was a "mongrel" and that the world
ahead of him would be a hard one. As Jerry-B leaves Powderjay
on his first venture into the world, Red-Rusty reminds him: "You
are a Mongrel, Jerry-B Boneyard. You will have to prove your-
self. When people look at you they won't want you. You're such
an ugly dog" (p. 53). Jerry-B, who carries this warning with
him, begins to glory in his toughness as a mongrel—he deter-
mines to be a self-made dog. At each home his name grows
longer as he endures and survives various hardships, and the ex-
panding mongrel name takes on an heraldic character. When the
great cycle of his adventures brings him once again to the Pow-

derjay household, he listens proudly to Shan Powderjay's praise of his stoic virtue: "He's had it hard in the dog world; so hard that he has become toughened to it. He can stand more than any dog I know; Jerry-B Boneyard has pluck." Jerry-B bristles with pleasure at this praise from one of his sharp critics: " 'Mongrel Mettle' I wanted to say but didn't" (p. 185).

Filled with pride in his mongrelism, Jerry-B meets the beautiful bitch, Dossie:

> "Would you marry a mongrel, Dossie?" I asked. "You haven't asked me my name but I am Jerry-B Boneyard Powderjay Dodderidge Fox Hammonds Lakin Hammertight Blevins Doore, the Mongrel!"
> "If I loved a mongrel, I would marry him," she replied. "But tell me how did a mongrel get a name as fine as you have? It sounds to me like a pedigreed name."
> "I have made my own name in the world," I said proudly. (p. 197)

Brandishing his splendid name like a shining lance, Jerry-B plunges into a courtship of Dossie and wins her hand. The mongrel has won against great odds and has thus prepared himself for his big curtain speech.

> But I was fulfilling one thing; I was a mongrel marrying a pedigreed lady. I was helping to mix the dogs of America and make them a Democratic Race of Dogs, one that would become powerful as a race of dogs in our future that was to be. I thought of this as I trotted beside my true-love Dossie toward the sunrise of an August morning that promised to be a fair day for love, security, and a more democratic World of Dogs. (p. 201)

With this mock romantic flourish, Stuart ends his story, which remains primarily a dog story despite the satirical overtones mentioned above. A close reading makes it clear that the satire derived naturally from the mongrel situation and remained a secondary matter for the author. He did not set out to write a treatise on the racial question. Critics who read this primarily as a manifesto on the racial ills of the world are simply influenced by the current temper of the times. This little book is not a companion piece to Orwell's *Animal Farm;* it is more in the order of Jack London's *Call of the Wild.* Stuart is an artist, not a propagandist. Nevertheless, because of its fable quality, it exerts an appeal in the swift-moving world of Jerry-B Boneyard. *Mongrel Mettle* will always remain one of the most delightful of Stuart's minor works.

II Hie to the Hunters

Mark Twain, living through the crass days of the Great Barbecue following the Civil War, observing the venality of the great financiers and feeling middle age come on him, turned several times in his work to the "peaceful valley" of his childhood as it still lived in his imagination. *Tom Sawyer* represented an excursion, as did many scenes in the first half of Twain's *Old Times on the Mississippi*. Stuart, an admirer of Twain, in *Hie to the Hunters* so idyllically portrays his own "peaceful valley" that the book becomes in effect a beautiful agrarian hymn.

To catch the inner form of this novel, it is, therefore, best to conceive of it as a prose poem. Critics have been arguing for some time now that the reason poetic epics are no longer written is that the poetic imagination is now going into poetic novels. The structure, mood, and tone of this novel mark it as a kind of poetic fable, or as a kind of hymn to nature and the earth. There is a curious combination of factuality (how to strip tobacco) and fantasy (Bill Hargis as a kind of fairy-tale villain almost instantaneously changed at the end to a virtuous defender of Peg Sparks' burning barn) that gives the story an air of fable. The physical scenes are usually preternaturally bright and clear. The two boys Jud Sparks, or "Sparkie," and Didway Hargis, "Did," live out their country idyll in a world of sharp, vivid colors. Their food has a luscious, country savor; and the bell tones of the fox hounds carry over the lonesome mountains to the snug barn loft where Sparkie and Did sleep, burrowed in sweet smelling hay. To a Northern sociologist this area would be "hillbilly" land, but to Jesse Stuart it is the "Golden Book of W-Hollow," as pristinely and poetically beautiful for him as the childhood Wales of Dylan Thomas's imagination.

The opening scene of the action is pure Tom Sawyer, and we might as well take it as such. Tough mountain-boy Jud Sparks saves the scrawny city rich-boy, Didway Hargis, from two bullies who are beating him. Sparkie invites Did to come home and live with him, promising to protect him and to teach him hunting and shooting. Did finds a good home with Peg and Arn, Sparkie's stepfather and mother, respectively. The two boys sleep in the barn, hunt, cut wood, trap, plow, and do all thing together; Did, the city boy, gradually becomes tough and strong, and grows to love the country immensely. From time to time Did's parents appear, trying to compel him to return to them. The hill people take to Did; and eventually there is a mass fight at night in a corn field, between the people of Plum Grove, defending Did's choice, and the people of Greenwood, helping Did's father. Greenwood is defeated.

At the same time, the hill people are caught in a feud between tobacco growers and fox hunters. Fox hounds are being poisoned and tobacco barns burned, and no one know how to placate the two sides. The climax comes when the barn-burner sets fire to the barn in which Did and Sparkie sleep. The sheriff, Bill Hargis, and fifty men from Greenwood arrive to help put out the fire. Did and Sparkie catch the barn-burner, "Brier-Patch Tom" Eversole, who confesses not only to burning the barns but also to poisoning the dogs. Thus the breach is healed between the town and country folk and between fox hunters and tobacco men, and Did comes to terms with his father. The novel ends with a Christmas scene in which the Sparks family rejoice over their finest Christmas, the best gift being a new artificial leg for Peg, who can now discard his wooden one. As the last scene closes, we learn that Sparkie will not go to school but will remain always on the land to which he is so attached. Did will return and finish high school but will eventually return to the land which he now loves almost as much as Sparkie does.

This basic plot is merely the excuse that supports Stuart's poetic fable of the land. The poetry comes through in the set pieces describing the beauty of the hunt, the fields, the corn-shucking night, and other rural scenes. This poetic quality is implicit in the scene where Sparkie and Did awaken in the barn loft in the morning and hear all the animal life of the farm awaken, stir, and chatter in the great morning hymn of life:

> When Peg's lantern came to the barn at this hour and his wooden leg sounded against the frozen ground, every living thing around the barn awakened. Did heard, above the music of the roosters, Dick and Dinah stand up in their stalls and bray. He heard the popping of knee joints as the cattle arose in their stalls. The hungry fattening hogs spoke to Peg with wheezing

grunts. Even Shooting Star and Lightning spoke with pleasant whines and Fleet and Thunderbolt answered them from their kennels.[3]

Or the corn-shucking scene, a bright moonlit hymn to autumn fruitfulness and fertility:

> The moon was high and bright. When a rabbit or a mouse ran from a shock of fodder, the shuckers could see him take off in the moonlight. This was the night of all nights, when there was the rustle of the dry fodder blade, and the ears of white and red corn were constantly in the air sailing to little heaps, while lovers lips met across the buff-colored fodder blades. This was a night of love and October mellowness, when the ears of corn, fodder blade, and leaf were ripened by the frosts, and the pumpkins yellow, brown, and golden, lay over the big cornfield. (p. 155)

Although the narrative point of view is third-person omniscient, the viewer frequently goes into the consciousness of Did to show the weather as a backdrop and as a brightness to this world of Plum Grove. Did, who has much of the poetic sensitivity of his creator, Jesse Stuart, makes a prime viewer of the natural beauty of the world. This whole stream of poetic life reaches its highest point in a kind of Wordsworthian pantheism when Did, learning to plow on one of the great open mountain slopes in the brisk, life-giving November wind, has an intense realization of the animate life of the earth and hurls himself prone in an ecstasy of identification. This lyric thrust which has been building to this scene and has its apogee here—has the kind of nature mysticism which English poetry has been noted for through Andrew Marvell, Henry Vaughan, William Blake, William Wordsworth, and others:

> On the fifth day Did looked out over the great dark bread-loaf mountains with tall upturned teacup-shaped peaks that jotted the ridge line against the sky. The great sweeps of bright brisk wind that blew through the pine needles on the mountain and the teacup-peaks swept over the dark upturned loam that Did Hargis had plowed. Did walked between the handles of his plow and breathed this wind. He swelled his chest as he breathed the good wind more deeply than he had ever breathed before. The rugged beauty of this earth . . . had done something to him. . . . caused him to love life more than ever before; caused him to want to live forever. . . .

This earth is a great living body, Did thought as he stretched his body on the plowed ground and put his ear against the earth. There must be great rivers running underground that are its veins and arteries and it must have a heart. . . .

He lay there with his ear against the ground and listened for the pounding of the earth's heart. . . . I hear the earth's heart, he thought. It almost lifts me up. I will shout to Peg and Sparkie and tell them what I have found! . . . His heart was the heart beating for the world, his blood was the blood of the world, his words were the dirt words speaking for the world. (pp. 192-4)

As a craftsman, Stuart realizes that the text can tolerate only a certain amount of this lyricism without cloying. He needs a contrast to heighten its effectiveness; and he gets it with what might be called the pragmatics of the book, or the "how-to-do-it" series. In other words, we turn from pantheism to the factuality of "how to fell a tree," "how to plow a field," "how to run a trap-line," and how to perform a dozen other farm tasks. These "how-to" scenes serve several purposes: they not only provide a needed counterpoint to the lyricizing, but have a nostalgic charm for the city-bred audience. Taken together these scenes constitute a sequence which shows how Did Hargis becomes pragmatic man, one who masters his environment and becomes strong, self-reliant, and self-supporting. They invert another American prototype, the Horatio Alger story which showed the poor country boy making his way with pluck and work to riches in the city: Did is the poor little rich boy of the city, bullied and physically weak, who makes his way with pluck and energy to riches of health and strength and happiness in the country.

As might be expected, the pragmatic scenes are narrated in a simple, direct manner that makes them delightful to read as separate experiences even apart from the totality of the action described. For example, the scenes describing Sparkie and Did setting out their traps and Did's later running of the trap line have been reprinted as a short story and included in Stuart's volume *Save Every Lamb* (pp. 70-80, 95-106).

Equally important in establishing our empathy with the world of *Hie to the Hunters* is the categorizing of the characters into familiar types. Sparkie, for instance, is an example of the "Natural Man" of romantic primitivism. He is untutored in books and the sophisticated knowledge of the cities, but he possesses much of the lore of the land and forests, and he has to some degree the "knowledge carried to the heart" which Allan Tate has found more domesticated in agrarian than in urban culture. At the end, Sparkie has made his decision to stay with the land and to forego school. He will remain always the "Natural Man." Sparkie exemplifies still another type, for he resembles Huck Finn. Like Huck he is rough, untutored, unschooled; and some of his actions (making bootleg liquor and selling it in town) get him talked about by the town people, who regard him much as Tom Sawyer's folks regarded Huck Finn. Like Huck, Sparkie loves a free, wild life and objects to all restraint; and, like Huck, he has a natural love of justice for the underdog and will do anything he can to get it for him.

Did Hargis as a type is the poor little rich boy who runs away to the country to find himself.[4] When he goes in search of life, he finds it deep within himself while laboring behind a plow on the windswept uplands of a Kentucky mountainside. Did brings city culture with him, and compares city with country culture to the disparagement of the former. For instance, he admires the *real logs* burning in Peg's fireplace; in town Did's parents have artificial logs with gas jets. Did takes to the tobacco-growing, fox-hunting life of Sparkie and blends his own life with it. In this sense, city culture is portrayed as a pseudo-culture, and the implication is that it is greatly inferior to Sparkie's mountain culture. Did is like Jesse Stuart in combining book culture with mountain culture, but he starts from book culture and works toward the outdoor world whereas Stuart in his own life reversed this order. In his sensitivity and his poetic nature, Did resembles Stuart, who undoubtedly projects some of his own traits into Did. Did is reborn into life and nature, and in attaining his new knowledge he becomes the "happy man" in Stuart's pantheon.

Did's father, Bill Hargis, emerges as a type figure also: the prim, prissy "cityite" who is weak in the legs, prances about mouthing platitudes, and equates excellence with affluence. In the barn-burning scene at the end of the book, Bill, after a brief and unconvincing struggle with himself, comes to the aid of Peg and the men who are saving Peg's barn. Bill "sees the light," is reunited with Did, and magnanimously allows Did to make his own decision. Bill remains so much the type figure that he never comes alive, but curiously enough he does no great harm to the book. Sparkie and Did are alive enough to carry the story, and

Bill is like a Punch and Judy figure who makes a brief appearance full of sound and fury and then disappears without anyone regretting it.

Allied to this typing is the dim appearance of the rebirth archtype—one of Stuart's favorites—in Did's rebirth at the end of the book. Leaving home, family, and town, Did undergoes a trial or testing period and emerges successful and victorious, a "new" man. Even the great fox hound, Thunderbolt, who is poisoned by "Brier Patch" Tom, is in a sense reborn in the tiny pup that struggles out of Thunderbolt's kennel to greet Sparkie in the closing scene of the book.

Readers familiar with Stuart's early short stories, those published in the 1930's, will be aware that Stuart has toned down the mountain dialect greatly. Instead of the exuberant idiom of "Battle Keaton Dies," we find a simple, clear narrative style with enough dialect words to give us the flavor of the Plum Grove milieu. Sparkie and his father constantly use the expression "It's suspicy" (p. 43) when they suspect something underhand. Sparkie leads Did early in the morning to the ice-covered wash basin with the remark, "We'd better dabble, Did. . . . It'll wake all the sleep left in us!" (p. 49). The engaging use of "dabble," for "wash" runs throughout the book. Equally graphic is the use of the Southern dialect verb "sull": "Bill Hargis sat sulled like a possum while his wife smiled, tapping her feet to the music" (p. 185).

A number of the idioms Stuart employs to give pungency to the narrative are well-established folk usages. Arn, for instance, calls the boys in to a huge country breakfast of eggs, ham, gravy, hot biscuits, butter, fried potatoes, sorghum molasses, and wild grape jelly: "Ye boys git your feet under the table. . . . I've got ye a breakfast that'll stick to your ribs" (p. 50). The idiom, "that'll stick to your ribs," has been heard in the rural South for many generations, as well as the idiom, "As well as common" (p. 128), which is Peg's reply to Sheriff Watkins query, "Mr. Sparks. . . . How are you?" Such idioms convey the flavor of a time and of a people with an immediacy that no purely verbal description can duplicate. One of Stuart's greatest strengths as a writer is his ear for the homely, pungent idiom of his people.

The story of *Hie to the Hunters* is a slight one; the mood is light. The reader closes the book aware that he has read a simple morality play in which "knowledge carried to the heart" triumphs over the pseudo-culture of the cities. It is idyllic, but it is back-boned with actuality, the kind that Stuart picked up from living forty-odd years in W-Hollow. A clean, mountain wind sweeps through the whole book, immensely invigorating. Vicariously we enter into the lives of the two hunters Sparkie and Did as they course over the mountains in their hunts, and hail them as joy-ously as Arn, who shouted, "Hie to the hunters," and watched them gallop away. This high-spirited, joyous memory of a clean land and a clean people is what we carry with us as we close the book.

III   The Good Spirit of Laurel Ridge

In *The Good Spirit of Laurel Ridge* Stuart constructed a one-man novel or novelette based on the fictional Theopolis ("Op") Akers. The real life model for Op Akers is George Alexander, a long-time resident of W-Hollow, and, according to Stuart, "a real life Henry David Thoreau." In the same article Stuart adds that "George is more on my pages that any other character be-cause he's the greatest."[5] Op completely dominates the novel; the story moves well when he is on stage, but it suffers drastically when the camera cuts away from Op to pick up one of the six or seven minor characters that cluster about him. They have little life, and the fact that Stuart seems to have little concern for or interest in them, comes through clearly to the readers. The critics were mixed in their reception of this novel, some praising it as a richly textured study of folklore, others damning it because of a flimsy plot. Yet the novel was rather widely printed and en-joyed some success in Europe.

The plot line of the story is simple enough. Old Op Akers, long-time squatter on wooded Laurel Ridge, is waiting to see if an eye operation has restored his vision. Lucretia, a young girl who claims to be his daughter, is living with him and caring for him in his blindness. The operation is successful; and Op, able to see again, takes up his life once more as a man who lives completely on what the forests and streams yield. Lucretia, although she is a city girl from Akron, continues to live with Op and is courted alternately by a hillbilly Romeo, Hootbird Hammertight, and by a blond, bearded young man who hides out in the mountains and pretends to be the spirit of Ted Newsome, a mountaineer who was murdered thirty years before. Op says, "Ted's a good spirit"; on the surface at least he is the "good spirit of Laurel Ridge." Op, who has lived for years as the solitary inhabitant of Laurel Ridge, suddenly finds himself overwhelmed when Alfred and Julia Pruitt arrive from Akron and ask to be taken in. Alf, a city man and cousin of Op's daughter Lucretia, has a neurotic fear that the cities of the world are all going to be burned by the atomic bomb. Op, much against his will, puts Alf and Julia in his smoke-house; then he sets about making a man of Alf—that is, making him capable of sustaining himself in the primitive world of Laurel Ridge.

Complications arise when Hootbird gets jealous of the bearded man's attentions to Lucretia and sets out to capture the "Spirit." All the fox hunters of the region are also after the spirit and threatening to hang him because he has been killing and eating their foxes. Alf suffers while trying to keep up with Op in long walks through snake-infested woods and in daily heats with the hoe in Op's garden. Op's primitive world is further outraged when an army jeep appears with four soldiers searching for Rodney Bohannon, an AWOL soldier. It is the first appearance of an automobile on Laurel Ridge. A much more welcome visitor is Op's childminded son, Run-Around Jack, who returns from winter farmwork in the Middle West to catch butterflies, his yearly avocation during the summer months.

The climax comes with the capture of the wild man who has been masquerading as Ted Newsome. The fox hunters and Hootbird are preparing to hang him, despite Op's and Lucretia's protest, when Jack brings the jeep-load of soldiers in time to prevent the hanging and to disclose that the wild man is really Rodney Bohannon, who has been hiding out because he erroneously believes that he is guilty of murder. Bohannon is taken off to serve his six-month sentence. Lucretia is in love with Rodney, and Op gladly sends her away to marry him; Alf and Julia, overcome with the rigors of Laurel Ridge life, have already departed. Jack will leave with the coming of the fall. The wildness and solitude Op loved has returned to Laurel Ridge. He is again content; for the omnicompetent man, solitude is a blessing not a curse.

The Good Spirit of Laurel Ridge, undoubtedly a minor novel with certain obvious deficiencies, has an appeal which needs to be accounted for. If we had to name the source of this appeal, we would call it Romantic primitivism. Op Akers is a fairly close approximation to the "child of nature" beloved by Rousseau and Wordsworth. Laurel Ridge becomes a kind of primitive rural Eden secure from the loud alarms of the world. The city man today, choking on the polluted air of the great metropolis, can escape with Op to Laurel Ridge where the white clouds float below the ridge-top and the clean winds sweep up through miles of forest. Op is even more self-sufficient than Henry David Thoreau was on Walden Pond; for Op is the omnicompetent man who provides for all his needs in a life of primitive simplicity.

"Is Op a varmint or a man?"[6] Alf Pruitt questions as he looks at Op's hairy body stripped for swimming. This query comes to the mind of most of the city-dwellers in the book when they encounter Op, for they have never seen such simplicity combined with such knowledgeability of the earth—to them Op seems like a canny animal. But Op, in his own way, is a wise one; and he states the Edenesque theme early when he says, "There are still pockets of the earth left as God made 'em . . . Fruit, nuts, and wild game left as they must have been in the beginnin'. Laurel Ridge is one of these places" (p. 74). Moreover, this rural Eden is proof of the hand of a beneficent God behind the nature that Op loves: "There's a weed a-growin' on Laurel Ridge fer every ailment of the body. The Old Master has a purpose for every weed and flower he's created!" (p. 91). Op's vision of the land remains that of virgin soil uncontaminated by exploitation; by nature it produces herbs, a natural function and the norm that should be followed. Alf Pruitt, the serpent in this Eden, grows greedy looking at the richness of this virgin soil. When Alf proposes to take off the timber and put the land under cultivation, Op scorns him for not realizing nature's beneficent provisions:

> "And, Alf, ye don't haf to raise corn and have cattle here. There's enough wild game to furnish a body meat. Enough nuts on these trees to take the place of corn. The kernels from the black walnut and butternut are sweeter'n the kernels from corn! Why work and dig and tear up somethin' God Almighty has made, when there's no use to it? This won't be my land anymore when its torn up and destroyed."
>
> "But it's not your land now," Alf reminded him. "You told me it belonged to Snake Blue."
>
> *"He's got the deed on paper,"* Op said. *"I've got the deed for it in my heart.* I own this land more'n anybody else." [*emphasis added*]

This last statement sounds more and more like the Transcendental doctrines of that Romantic primitivist Henry David Thoreau, who walked perceptively over the farms of his Walden neighbors, drinking in the beauty of line and color and shadow and all the joy which exuded from the fresh earth. When he withdrew, he took with him infinite treasures of imagination locked within his mind, but the hard-fisted farmers who held title to the land thought he took no more with him than a few frost-bitten apples. Thoreau speaks of their lack of perception as scathingly as Op speaks of Alf Pruitt. Op luxuriates in this nature provided by the Old Master and seems in general to feel that his is the best of all possible worlds, although even he is hard put to explain the purpose of snakes in the grand design. "But I kill every kind of a snake. I can't say I like a-one: I've never learned why the Master put the water moccasin here unless it's to thin out the minners" (p. 130).

Op bears other resemblances to the more cultivated nineteenth-century Romantics. Like many of the English and American Romantics who believed in the superiority of all natural products over man-made products, Op had made an Aeolian Harp—not that he called it by such a fancy name. He had horsehairs fastened to wooden pegs set in the cabin wall; when the wind blew through the horsehairs, it made what Op called "horsehair music."

> I sit out here and lissen to it winter, spring, fall and summer. . . . And when I go to bed it oftens sings me to sleep. . . . A body can hear fiddles a-playin' if he lissens. . . . he can hear mandolins, geetars, dulcimers, and harps, too. Hear 'em all a-playin' together. . . . I could sit here fer the next hour and tell ye tunes I've heard played on these cabin walls. (pp. 20-22)

"Natural Music" is as good, or better, than man-made music.

To complete our gallery of Romantic primitives we have Op's mentally retarded son, Run-Around Jack. Jack is a free spirit, an eternal child, a Peter Pan of the uplands who exults in the beauty of the outdoors, has no guile, would harm no one, and pursues an eternal vision of beauty in butterflies which he catches and admires and then releases. Op, who loves Jack, tells us:

> Jack can't kill, he's too gentle. He's got the mind and heart of a child. A happy child, too. . . . All of this land is his home. . . . he'll ketch butterflies all summer. . . . Here on Laurel Ridge Jack

has his freedom. Here up near the sky is the best home Jack can ever have. People understand him up here. They know he wouldn't harm even a butterfly. (pp. 119-200)

Summarily speaking then, Stuart has constructed for us an idyllic pastoral where the simple, agrarian life of the past century is telescoped with the technological life of the present day. William Empson argues in his book *English Pastoral Poetry* (published in England under the title *Some Versions of Pastoral*), that the fundamental strategy of the pastoral is an acting out of the biblical injunction "The last shall be first": that is, the pastoral shows that the simple people of this world, who possess neither class status nor wealth, and are thus "the last" in one sense, do possess a wisdom and goodness which make them first in a moral sense. This is another way of describing the Romantic primitivism of *The Good Spirit of Laurel Ridge*, since Op, untutored and uncouth by the world's standards, is yet far superior in terms of survival capability to Alf Pruitt, the neurotic weakling who flees in fear from the city, who is cared for by Op, and who then flies back to the mixed comforts, fears, and pollutions of the city. Thus Op, our child of nature, is closely related to Wordsworth's "Michael" and "The Leech-gatherer on the Moor"—and Run-Around Jack, to Wordsworth's "Idiot Boy." Op never heard of Wordsworth's romantic observation that "Nature never did betray the heart that loved her," but, if it were explained to Op in his own language, he would have agreed heartily. The whole novel, in fact, is a fable in support of this nature-as-norm thesis.

But Stuart never bogs down in any overwrought attitudinizing. Op is a thoroughly earthy character and an aura of humor hangs about him whether he is mulling over the "Adam bumb" that Alf Pruitt's told him about; scornfully dismissing the cowardly Hootbird Hammertight, "Boy's got all the guts of a grasshopper" (p. 63); or coining a metaphor when he observes in the midst of a gunfight that Ben Hammertight's ". . . . too slow to catch a stud turtle" (p. 182). The humor is, for the most part, of the rough, obvious frontier type that thrives on exaggeration and eccentric images. Op talks much, for instance, about his idea of immortality—to return as a spirit and swim around in the air above Laurel Ridge.

A lot of people I want to float over like a big chicken hawk, pumping my wings just a little and kicking the bright air with

my feet like I'm a-swimmin' up there above 'em. Yep, I want to
scare the mortal hell outten a few people. Old Doshie's one. I'll
make 'er think 'er little short legs are a-ailin' 'er. . . . I'll dive at
'er all the way from Honeywell to Wince Leffard Gap. ((p. 43-
14)

The spirits are very real for Op; as he passes one day to look at
foundation stones where a church once stood, he sees in his
mind's eye a lumberjack at an old-time revival carried kicking
and squealing to the church altar to confess. "Then everybody
watched him as he laid his sins upon the altar. They lissened to
his confession, which was allus something to hear when a lumberjack, ore digger or a collier confessed" (p. 64).

Op pauses in his hoeing one day to tell Alf and Julia Pruitt
about the time his brother Adger, disguised in a white nightgown,
beard, and long hair appeared as Christ one night at the Free-
will Baptist Church, in the middle of a big revival.

> "Oh, Lord," Brother Smallwood said, "come down from heaven
> and be with us tonight. Come. . . . right down through the ceil-
> ing. We don't mind, Lord. We'll repair the roof." And, about
> that time Brother Adger, who was a-standin' in the back of the
> church house beside the door . . . said: "Wouldn't it be better to
> wall in at the door, Brother Smallwood?"
> ". . . No need to tear up the roof and ceiling" . . . Brother Adger
> said. "I don't approve of a lot of extra work fer nothin'." At that,
> Boadie Sloas, a terrible sinner but under conviction, went out
> the winder headfirst, with Jim Pennix, Hester Creamans, and
> Jimmy Overton a-followin'. . . . Wimmen run out the door
> screamin'. Little younguns woke up from their sleep and ran
> atter their mothers.
> But Brother Sweeter Barnhill, Sister Shug Meadows, Ossie and
> Tillie Redfern, Bill and Brusie Flannigan come with their arms
> lifted and fell at Brother Adger's feet. . . . (pp. 156-7)

When a birthmark on Brother Adger's cheek finally betrays him,
he is haled into court; and his pap has to pay a costly fine to get
him released. All during the trial Adger could give only one ex-
planation of his impersonation: "I wanted to see whether they
really did want the Lord, Our Saviour, to visit 'em or not" (p.
158).

This humor comes to a climax in Op's exuberant account of
the night he rode the devil home. Op tells the skeptical Alf, who

grows fearful during the tale, how he was possum hunting one night and took a huge drink of persimmon brandy. He woke up two nights later lying flat on his back with his eye sockets filled with rain water. The devil appeared, huge, horned, with skin like a bear's and offered Op a ride home. Op, afraid to refuse, climbed on the devil's shoulders. The devil started trotting, then galloped, then began racking. Thunder and lightning rumbled through the forest. "'How do you like yer ride?' said the devil . . . 'I love rackin',' I said" (p. 217). The storm grew worse; great trees fell splintered in the forest; but the devil stayed just ahead of the storm until he skidded to a stop in front of Op's cabin and kicked a giant cloven hoof at Op's barking dog. "'If ye kick that dog I'll dehorn ye,'" I said. . . . I didn't thank the devil for my ride. To hell with him, I thought, that's a friendship that can't do me no good" (pp. 218-9). The wild folk humor running through the whole account is irresistible; moreover, it matches well Op's character as a child of nature.

But the book was raked over the coals by a number of critics, primarily because Stuart's real interest was in Op Akers, the poor man's Henry David Thoreau, and because the minor characters exist as mere fillers; the reader soon becomes aware of the author's lack of interest in his lesser creatures. The mountain people—Doshie, Hootbird, and Ben Hammertight—come off better than the city people—Lutie, Rodney Bohannon, Alf and Julia Pruitt. For instance, the speech of the mountain people is realistic, but the others speak in a completely stilted fashion. Lieutenant Cox engages in a conversation with Op which sounds natural enough when Op speaks, but the lieutenant's language is as wooden as that in an amateur's first play (pp. 227-30). The plot climax is pretty much ruined for this reason. The climax brings a confrontation between Private Bohannon and Lieutenant Cox, but their speech is so wooden and unconvincing, and in such sharp contrast to the pungent, homely phrases of Op Akers, that all illusion of reality is pretty much dissipated (pp. 256-61). Equally unconvincing is the strained use of coincidence; Rodney Bohannon, for instance, just *happens* to look like the long dead Ted Newsome; and, to pile coincidence on coincidence, he just *happens* to have picked, from all of the hundreds of tombstones in the Freewill Baptist Churchyard, the stone of Ted Newsome as the source of his assumed name. These defects, plus the fact that Ted Newsome's off-stage appearances are too obviously manipulated as a "suspense" device, led Carl Carmer, in an otherwise favorable review in the New York *Herald Tribune,* to damn the "flimsy and trite plot."

All in all, the book is too stagey and labored. Furthermore, it is so episodic (fifty-seven episodes in two hundred and sixty-one pages) that it distracts the reader. We have the feeling that this is ideal material for one of Stuart's short stories but that it cannot support the novelette form in which it is cast. There is one other possibility. Stuart could have put the Op Akers material into a series of sharp autobiographical vignettes, deleting the distracting and imperfect minor characters. In form these would have been something like a small-scale *Death Comes for the Archbishop,* and they would have been good.

The problem about this parable of Romantic primitivism is identifying the good spirit of Laurel Ridge. Although Op says it is Ted Newsome, the reader may feel in closing the book that Op Akers himself is the spirit; and a considerable case could be made for him. Or it may be that Stuart intends a kind of secondary symbolism, implying that the exuberant energy that whelms up from nature and suffuses the entire book and Op in particular is the real good spirit of Laurel Ridge. At least this proliferating sense of nature is what remains longest with the reader.

IV Daughter of the Legend

Early in his writing career Stuart wrote a brief novel based on the Melungeons, an obscure people of mixed race living in the eastern mountains of Tennessee. He first learned of the Melungeons during his college years at Lincoln Memorial Institute. Since folklore held that the Melungeons mingled Negro blood with their white and Indian blood, they were discriminated against by white people. Their real tragedy was exemplified for Stuart by an incident he ran across in one town where the Melungeons were barred from the white school because of Negro blood and from the Negro school because of being too white. Moved by their plight, Stuart constructed a novel, *Daughter of the Legend,* which attacked racial segregation as it told the story of Deutsia Huntoon, the beautiful Melungeon. He put the manuscript aside for years and finally completed and published it in 1965. It had a poor critical reception and is not one of his better novels. To understand the critics' disfavor, we must consider the story.

When Dave Stoneking, a lumberjack from Virginia, comes into eastern Tennessee to cut a plot of timber, he meets and falls in love with Deutsia Huntoon, a beautiful Melungeon girl. He marries her, knowing quite well that he will be proscribed by the town of Oak Hill and by all of the white people of Cantwell County. His closest personal friend, Ben Dewberry, turns against him, as does Fern Hailston, Ben's fiancée. In spite of this prejudice, David builds a strong log cabin home for his wife on Sanctuary Mountain, the refuge of the Melungeons and a place of great natural beauty; there they rejoice in their love for each other. Dave is a fine cabinet maker and their life seems idyllic—as long as they stay on the mountain.

When Dave goes into Oak Hill, he is not allowed to eat in the restaurant because he has become one of the Melungeons. Deutsia is soon expecting a child, and they pass a fine Christmas with her family. As Deutsia's time draws near, she grows more somber; and there is a hint of some coming catastrophe. When the great spring equinoctial storms come, Deutsia's baby is born; but the mother dies of a massive hemorrhage. Dave is overcome with grief; and, four days after his wife's burial, he takes a last look around his mountain home and gives the key to his mother-in-law. He leaves his son with his mother-in-law, knowing that the child should stay with the Melungeons and grow up with them. Dave walks away toward the valley, where he boards a bus that will return him to his own people in Virginia.

This poor novel, one which Stuart probably should not have published, has a very limited scope; it seems more like an inflated short story. Compared to *Taps For Private Tussie*, the present novel is flat, humorless, and strained. There is an earnestness about it which seems to derive from the fact that it is a "message" book—on the wickedness of racial segregation. Although Stuart seems to feel that the validity of his message insures the quality of his novel, the novel fails—even if read primarily as a tract. The failure lies in the artificiality of the characters, especially of Deutsia Huntoon, who remains a one-dimensional character throughout. Deutsia's family march on stage with a congeries of strange names—Daid, Meese, Alona, Pribble, Force, Cress, and Bass—but these names cannot individualize them. They remain puppets. Only a couple of the minor characters,

Skinny and Sylvania (imported from Stuart's short story "Sylvania Is Dead") strike sparks of vitality. The breakdown in characterization is the key to the novel's failure. We are told of Deutsia's beauty (physically she looks a good deal like Subrinea Tussie of *Trees of Heaven*) and her desirability, but she never comes alive.

Stuart also made a fundamental error in this novel in making it a romantic story. He has never been at ease in treating romantic love, and he is not primarily a thesis writer. When he puts both love and a thesis into the same novel, he is hopelessly lost and self-conscious. Ordinarily, the dialogue in Stuart's fiction is carefree, spontaneous, and natural; but in *Daughter of the Legend* we find some of the stiffest dialogue outside Fenimore Cooper's Leatherstocking Tales: " 'It should take only two people to decide on whether or not to get married,' Deutsia said. 'Just you and I' " (p. 111). Deutsia as an untutored mountain girl should undoubtedly say—"Just you and me." And the language in which David Stoneking tells his story is rather highflown:

> "I've come to marry you," I said. "I want you more than anything in this world."
> We embraced. As lodestone is to metal we were drawn together by an irresistible force called love. (p. 111)

> "Dave there is something I want to tell you." Deutsia said turning her eye from the flaming fire. "I'm going to give you a present next spring. . . . [Stuart's ellipsis] I mean it, Dave," she said. . . .
> "Oh, that's the best news yet!" I said. "I'm really going to kiss you for this good news."
> Before the fire. . . . I pulled her carefully over to me, her face beneath mine, her hair streaming down to the floor, and I bent over until my lips met her lips. I held her there and kissed her fondly while the light of the dancing flames flickered over her hair and the dry wood crackled. (p. 149)

Daughter of the Legend is clearly a novel which Stuart wrote without considering his limitations. He is a writer of great talent, but he should stick to the W-Hollow locale for his fiction. We think of what happened to William Faulkner when he left his Yoknapatawpha County to go to France in *The Fable*: he produced his windiest, poorest novel. Stuart, leaving W-Hollow and its milieu for the first time in his literary career, produced his poorest novel.

V Mr. Gallion's School

In 1967, Stuart published *Mr. Gallion's School*, an episodic novel, recounting the efforts of a forty-nine year old cardiac writer and ex-teacher to put Kensington High School back on its feet. George Gallion, principal, takes over a school riddled with theft, defiance, and defeatism; gradually in the course of a year he brings order, affection, and an honorable pride back to both students and faculty. At the conclusion of the novel, George finds he must resign because his heart is acting up, but he has put his educational house in order. He has guarded hopes of appointing a successor who will continue his reforms.

Such a book inevitably invites comparison with Stuart's earlier work on education, *The Thread That Runs So True*. In its concern with the plight of education in Kentucky, it is certainly a kind of *Thread* revisited. It must be said that the later book is not so good as the former. It lacks the freshness of *The Thread* . . . and most of all it lacks the "Folk." The dialogue of *Mr. Gallion's School* is trite and bookish—it is a somewhat labored replay of themes which Stuart did so much better in *The Thread*. . . . It lacks, too, the lyric freshness of the young teacher encountering his first problems in a world of mountains and great natural beauty.

Yet the book has its excellences. Stuart's passionate belief in education as America's only hope comes through as clearly as ever. His indictment of America's moral anemia, and his indictment of the parents of delinquents as the real villains of our contemporary ethical scene is harsh and convincing. Students, he observes, must be saved from their corrupt parents. He finds this corruption eminently represented by the hill elections where a hundred thousand dollars is spent to buy votes while furnaces in schools rust unrepaired and rickety floors threaten the lives of the students. The examples of this corruption are clear. Stuart inveighs here against a great enemy—one endemic throughout the nation. It is a noble cause and nobly intended, but the vehicle carrying his message is not his strongest. Lacking the pungent idiom of his earlier work, it leaves the reader with the regret that Stuart did not nurture this work longer before releasing it for publication.

CHAPTER 6

Elegist of a Lost World

JESSE STUART is a genuine, original, marvelously fecund writing man; and the unduly fretful twentieth century has not quite known what to do with him, how to classify him, what attitude to take towards him. As a result, it has so far evaded the questions, shaken its head, and refused to talk about him. But the world cannot ignore Jesse Stuart permanently, for he is a kind of great natural force, like Niagara Falls or Old Faithful. The function of the present study has been to lay out Stuart's work in its full scope and detail in order to overcome the bemusement of those who look away from him, and to give fuller information to those who have looked at him. Believing that Stuart is an author of genuine and lasting merit, I have also attempted a long range evaluation of his work and achievements as poet, fictionist, and autobiographer of a lost world.

Besides Stuart's four major volumes and one volume of juvenilia, there are several hundred poems which have been published in diverse magazines and never collected in book form. Since these uncollected poems show no new or divergent phases of the poet's talent, they need not prevent us from making certain summary judgments about his poetry. Stuart's poetry has been largely ignored by the "new critics"—by the Ransom, Tate, *Kenyon Review* disciples of densely packed, intellectualist, symbolist poetry—and it is easy enough to see why Stuart's work—lacking paradoxes, irony, and all the paraphernalia of the neo-metaphysical manner—would not appeal to this school. Yet the appeal of Stuart's poetry to a sizeable audience is an indisputable fact. Moreover, Max Eastman, John Hall Wheelock, Henry Seidel Canby, J. Donald Adams, Robert Hillyer, Robert Nathan, John G. Neihardt, W. H. Auden, Marianne Moore, Witter Bynner, Randall Jarrell and Frederick A. Pottle, chancellors of the acade-

my of American Poets and themselves all very distinguished
poets and critics, presented Stuart the Academy of American
Poets Award. Such a group would hardly bestow an award on
frivolous or second-rate poetry.

The critical neglect of Stuart is due, in part, to the fact that
criticism by its very nature yearns to categorize facts, to arrange
the likeminded together into matching groups, and Stuart seems
to resist such categorizing. He doesn't rest easily in any of the
conventional schools. The turn of his mind is indicated by the
American poets he espouses. In a letter to a fellow poet, he
picked Walt Whitman, Edgar Lee Masters, and Stephen Vincent
Benet as three figures who will be rehabilitated a century hence
to the status of leading poets.[1] He makes this critical judgment
somewhat defensively, knowing quite well that, with the excep-
tion of Whitman, it is out of the stream of critical opinion of the
present day. We feel very clearly in Stuart a sense of alienation
from the poets and critics of his own day. *The New Republic*
once published him with a group of Western poets, but Stuart
thinks of himself as a Southern poet and is chagrined that so few
critical anthologies treat him as such. One of the difficulties in
this respect may arise from the fact that Stuart derives very
strongly from the culture of the Appalachian region, which cannot be equated completely with Southern culture although there
is a definite overlap. A thorough study of the literary aspect of
the Appalachian culture is yet to be made. When it is done,
Stuart will emerge as one of the leading literary products of this
culture and perhaps will then lose much of his present sense of
alienation. (He has said that he sometimes feels like a man without a country because of his seeming exclusion from the cause
of Southern writers.)

But, in the final analysis, he will be judged more by his actual
poetry than by the remarks of his critics; and many good things
can be said about his poetry. It presents a gallery of interesting
and authentic mountain people who are earthy, not fake, folk;
and, now that Robert Frost is dead, Stuart seems to be the last
of living American poets with a genuine knowledge of an old
and vanished way of life, a way that he can make come alive in
his poetry without seeming to be synthetically folksy. Some of
his best poems have the springtime freshness of medieval lyrics.
He possesses sincerity and genuineness, and does not suffer
from the divided mind and the carefully nurtured ambivalences

of modern, intellectualist poetry. If he could embody this genuineness and sincerity in an idiom and language that would *fully* express it, he would be a great poet.

Among his defects as a poet is the fact that he has written too much. When the mood is on him, the poetry floods out. This compulsion seems so strong that it usually masters him; as a consequence, instead of revising poems, he is busy writing new ones. His ear for idiom is better in his short stories than in his poems, for in the latter he occasionally falls into a "poetic diction" that seems artificial and bookish, particularly when used about the robust people of the Plum Grove community. Pure lyricizing is his poorest vein. His best poems have some dramatic core to them, but he strikes the same tone, the same vein, too much. His attitudes toward life are few and soon stated; then he repeats them over and over. He has the vision and the spirit, but he has never compelled himself to the craft and concentration (as Yeats did in his later work) to articulate them completely. He does not achieve the inevitable phrase—it is not the nature of his work to be quotable; his lines will probably not enter future editions of *Bartlett's Quotations*. He is haunted by the specter of the poet he might have been.

Jesse Stuart—mountain poet, one of the Redskins (in Philip Rahv's phrase) of American poetry, a cultural primitivist, an anti-intellectual, a prober and chronicler of the Appalachians, the last American frontier—is an individualist; he belongs to no school. His individual pieces are marred and imperfect, but the totality of this poetic Appalachian world does indeed make a great impact on us. Who can imagine American literature without *The Spoon River Anthology*? Or without *Man with a bull-tongue Plow*? Stuart fills a niche in the hall of American poetry that was empty until he appeared. Out of W-Hollow and Plum Grove Churchyard he has done what all fine poets long to do: he has created a glory from the earth.

Nor has he been lacking as a fictionist. At this point in time, in fact, fiction seems his finest literary achievement. Stuart's real impact as a novelist and short story writer is greater now and will be even greater than present critics realize. Like William Faulkner, he is a natural writer who finds that his novels start out as short stories, and that his short stories all begin with some strong physical image. He is about as far away as we can get from the formalistic novelist; he is the impulse writer who follows his hunches. His story lies in his mind for a long time and then rises suddenly on a rush of language to coalesce around some unforgettable figure such as Battle Keaton or Uncle Jeff Powderjay. Stuart, a self-taught fictionist, drew on the memories of the lost world of his childhood and youth, making timeless vignettes in his fiction—Grandpa Tussie, Sid Tussie, Anse Bushman—characters who will live for a long time.

Stuart is the creator of a tiny postage stamp of soil, the fictional W-Hollow, and of the people who cluster there. There is a recognizable relationship of the real to the fictional W-Hollow, but the fictional one retains a fabulous quality. He is essentially a poetic fictionist who sees the real world but sees it lyrically. For this reason his finest poetic effects occur in his fiction. Seen through his fiction, W-Hollow takes on a kind of glow which belies the harshness of the mountain surroundings. He blends slice-of-life realism with a kind of Romantic primitivism and lyric exuberance which gives his work the flavor of a painting by Breugel the Elder or Grandma Moses. This exuberance comes through in big, strongly accented scenes which have great freshness and spontaneity. They are like great comic ballads in prose. His novels and short stories are thus strikingly original. We can see in them parallels to other writers, but nowhere is there an indication of any major influence.

A great part of Stuart's originality seems to derive from the degree to which his own strong personality infuses each story. Stuart has the potent sense of *self* possessed by many writers. It is not really egotism so much as a sense that his own being, consciousness, self, ego—call it what you will—functions at such a high frequency that it gives the impression of a great dynamo whirling at a vertiginous speed and generating enormous power. Stuart is not naïve at all, but it is so unusual today to meet a person who has maintained a childlike immediacy, freshness, and potency of ego (i.e., whose self has not been diluted or whittled away by concessions to the world) that many people on first meeting Stuart have the impression of naïveté. This immense dynamism of knowing, feeling, and assessing is an essential ingredient of his fictional success.

It is undoubtedly this potent awareness of self which accounts for Stuart's characteristic narrative stance. His inner energy overflows into his narratives; they bristle with action, move frequently in the present tense, are told in the first person—all devices to make us much more aware of the kinetic Stuart personality which infuses the story with drama. Realistic in their depiction of speech, customs, and place, they are often Romantic in their idealizing of the child as seer or their characterizing of the wisdom of the simple people of his world.

A fine mist of nature blows freshly out of all these stories. No other American writer today can call us so delightfully into the outdoor world. He constantly tells us that the wild life of earth gives us ultimate beauty. He shows us the tragedy of mountain gloom, but he also lets big themes shine through in a kind of joyous mountain glory which bears always the good bright light of Stuart's omnipresent humor. Essentially in his fiction he is a "yea-sayer," an affirmer. He enters empathically into the myriad human situations presented in his stories because he has an intrinsic interest in them as *human situations*. There is, aside from *Daughter of the Legend* and three or four early short stories, absolutely no didacticism or overt moralizing in his fiction.

There can, of course, be no doubt that Stuart's fiction belongs in the general category of Regionalism. He is part of that long line of American writers of place, dialect, and the outdoors who go back to A. B. Longstreet, Johnson Jones Hooper, and George Washington Harris in the nineteenth century and to Willa Cather, Ellen Glasgow, Elizabeth Madox Roberts, and William Faulkner in the twentieth. Stuart is, in fact, the regional writer par excellence, but he is not *just* a regional writer. Through W-Hollow and its people shine universals—a kind of unconscious welling up of stoicism, endurance, eternal laughter, love. We think, for instance, of how Huck Finn began in Mark Twain's memory of his childhood and ended as a many-sided symbol so moving to millions of different readers. So it is with Stuart's characters. And the region he has created—W-Hollow—has now taken its permanent place in the timeless geography of American fiction. It will keep its place there long after more fashionable writers of the present have faded completely away. The undoubted endurance of his creation is a prime measure of Stuart's accomplishment as a fictionist.

As the decade of the 1960's draws to a close, the shape and configuration of Stuart's life, which he has drawn so vigorously in the autobiographical works discussed earlier, emerges more and more clearly. Readers are impressed by his ineluctable commitment to education and democracy. These are not abstractions to him but living modes of being for which he has fought and agonized and been beaten and bloodied and exiled. No other single individual in the last thirty years has accomplished in this country so wide-scale an improvement of education as has Jesse Stuart.

Then there is Stuart the conservationist who loves the land, not only in his poetry and stories, but also in his life as a farmer who has planted hundreds of thousands of seedling pines, as a farmer who thinks of his land as entrusted to him for a few years and who is determined to improve it and hand it on richer and more beautiful to those who follow him. There is also Stuart the world ambassador who lectures in Egypt to the children of the ancient cultures of the Mediterranean basin and brings to them by a kind of connaturality the virtues of the New World. Altogether his shape and configuration as a writer and a person are unique.

Why do Stuart's autobiographical books still fascinate? The answer to this question provides a summary assessment of his work as an autobiographer. Stuart has the ability, absolutely essential to a good writer, to make everything he writes about himself, from a heart attack to a train ride or to teaching a class, come alive for the reader. More than this his own life is inherently dramatic. He embodies better than any other American writer the dual lives of a man of action and an artist. Added to this is the fabulous quality investing the pattern of his life. The poor mountain boy setting out for a mountain high school at the beginning of his public life is like poor Dick Whittington setting out for London and already destined to be lord mayor of London as Stuart was already destined to be an internationally famous writer. *How* he climbs the ladder of fortune makes eternally fascinating reading. *How* he fulfills the Horatio Alger myth of rags-to-riches endlessly attracts us.

The narrative style which he evolves brings his autobiographical work to life with pulsing vitality. *Beyond Dark Hills* wheels before us with quick, flashing scenes—swift moving and kaleidoscopic. The persona narrating the story has a kind of Adam-and-Eve freshness and sincerity which binds us close to the life being narrated. The flawless idiom of *God's Oddling* makes his father live for us as no other language could. What other book in American literature conveys the excitement and promise and real potentiality of teaching as does *The Thread That Runs So True?* More and more this country will learn that in Stuart it has produced one of its finest autobiographers.

How to sum up Jesse Stuart? In him we meet a trinity of nature, will, and individualism. The hills where his life rose live undyingly in his best work. His loving attention to those hills, both in his work and in his continued residence there, show how well he has conquered the strange disease of modern life. He holds everlastingly for the efficacy of the tiny, invisible, molecular moral forces that work from individual to individual and in time destroy the hardest monument of man's pride. From boyhood he has believed that one can do anything if he wants to badly enough. Today, at fifty-nine, he is running a prosperous thousand-acre farm, lecturing all over the country, teaching at a nearby university, taping lectures, answering all of a voluminous daily mail, working on four books, and writing poems and short stories. He is very much his own man. He will never succumb to Big Brother. He has always disdained the beaten path. More and more today it becomes evident that his works are the incarnation of a matchless individuality. That is why they will continue to live and do the world good.

Notes and References

Chapter One

1. *Beyond Dark Hills* (New York, 1938), p. 320.
2. Letter to Lee Oly Ramey, December 2, 1939, cited in note 1 of M.A. thesis of Lee Oly Ramey, "An Inquiry into the Life of Jesse Stuart as Related to His Literary Development and a Critical Study of His Works" (Ohio University, 1941), p. 189.
3. Ramey, p. 196.
4. *Beyond Dark Hills,* p. 40.
5. Quoted from a Stuart letter to the author, July 16, 1966, Athens, Greece.
6. *National Education Association Journal,* January, 1950.
7. *The Thread That Runs So True* (New York, 1949), p. 288.
8. *The Year of My Rebirth* (New York, 1956), p. 48.
9. *God's Oddling* (New York, 1960), quoted from the one-page preface, un-numbered.

Chapter Two

1. Letter from Stuart to the author, Greenup, Kentucky, August 17, 1962.
2. "An Autobiographical Reminiscence," *The University of Kansas City Review,* XXVII (October, 1960), 64.
3. *Ibid.,* 59.
4. *Ibid.*
5. She was a remarkable teacher. One day she patted Jesse on the head and said, "I'd like to live long enough to see what comes out of that head." "I'll never forget her," said Stuart. (Quoted from *J. Stuart Scrapbooks,* Item 233, Scrapbooks 51-60.)
6. *Beyond Dark Hills,* p. 58.
7. One hundred and fifty copies were printed. Only two of this original edition are now extant, one with Stuart and one with the University of Kentucky. The Council of the Southern Mountains, Inc., Berea, Kentucky, reproduced this in 1964 by offset printing from the pages of the original book.
8. Letter from Stuart to the author, Greenup, Kentucky, May 17, 1963.
9. *Harvest of Youth* (Howe, Oklahoma, 1930), p. 58.
10. "To Muddy Waters," "Batter Me Down, Life," and "My Love Will Remain When I Have Passed" became the untitled numbers 223-225 of *Man with a bull-tongue Plow* (New York, 1934). "My

Mountain Home" became number 232, and "To Edith" became number 236—retitled "To B. G."

11. Quoted from Hargis Westerfield, *"Harvest of Youth*, Stuart's First Published Book," *The American Book Collector*, XII, 6 (February, 1963), 23-24.

12. *Beyond Dark Hills*, p. 338.

13. Letter of Donald Davidson to Stringfellow Barr, June 3, 1933, quoted from Ramey, pp. 67-68.

14. *Beyond Dark Hills*, p. 387.

15. *Ibid.*, p. 393.

16. Stuart said in a talk at Princeton University (April 17, 1937) that at the time he wrote *Man with a bull-tongue Plow* he did not know how to scan verse. Quoted from Microfilm (Reel 1, Scrapbooks 1-20) of *Jesse Stuart Scrapbooks*.

17. Letter from Stuart to the author, Greenup, Kentucky, June 7, 1962.

18. Sonnet 541, *ibid.*, p. 278. This surrey image is repeated in Sonnet 544 and is quite effective, although it does not have the cold compactness of Emily Dickinson's famous carriage image in her poem, "Because I Could Not Stop for Death."

19. Sonnets 630-33, *ibid.*, pp. 322-24.

20. Sonnet 8, *ibid.*, p. 6.

21. Sonnets 412-16, *ibid.*, pp. 210-12.

22. *Head O' W-Hollow* (New York, 1936), pp. 6-23.

23. *Man with a bull-tongue Plow*, Sonnet 1, p. 3.

24. Some of Stuart's strangest poems are those in which the snakes speak up and describe their passionate love for each other, as in "Bull Blacksnake Speaks of Love and Fear" (p. 18).

Entwined with her [Lady Blacksnake] until our strength is spent
On warm spring moonless nights, our nights for love.
Her new spring skin against mine in the dark,
Her hard lips pressed to mine in evil night,
Our cold blood kindles to a fiery spark
As we embrace till dawn's chilly light.

25. *Album of Destiny* (New York, 1944), p. 164.

26. The author is indebted to Stuart for much background information about *Album of Destiny*, contained in letters from Stuart to the author.

27. She defines "pietas" as the sense of "the divine as it manifests itself in their [men's] communal life. Such an attitude is what the Romans called *pietas*, reverence before the gods and before one's ancestors." "The 'Pietas' of Southern Poetry," in *South: Modern Southern Literature in Its Cultural Setting*, Rubin and Jacobs, eds. (Garden City, N. Y., 1961), p. 99.

28. *Kentucky Is My Land* (New York, 1952).

29. There are a couple of exceptions to this. "One poem used in

this book, 'House in the Wind' was written when I was in Greenup High School . . . when I was 17 . . . it lay at the University of Kentucky where I had sent it to Professor Farquhar, who used to edit a magazine there. It was there, plus several others, for a number of years . . . And Oscar Sammons, a classmate, who later went there to college . . . looked up this poem for me and returned it. And years afterward I sent it to the *Yale Review* and it was accepted. Another old one is 'Desolation,' written in college." Quoted from a letter by Jesse Stuart (December 26, 1961, Greenup, Kentucky) to the author.

30. *Hold April* (New York, 1962), pp. 56-62.

31. *Ibid.*, p. 36. The last line of this poem seems the only weak line, as if Stuart put it in to complete the thought, even though it jars a little with the preceding lines.

Chapter Three

1. *Tales from the Plum Grove Hills* (New York, 1946), p. 181.
2. *Plowshare in Heaven* (New York, 1958), p. 138.
3. "Walk in the Moon Shadows," *ibid.*, p. 25.
4. *Men of the Mountains* (New York, 1941), p. 122.
5. *Ibid.*, p. 271.
6. Mary Louise Washington, "The Folklore of the Cumberlands as Reflected in the Writings of Jesse Stuart" lists seventy-odd pages of folk speech gleaned from Stuart's works (unpublished doctoral dissertation, Department of English, University of Pennsylvania, 1960).
7. *Tales from the Plum Grove Hills,* p. 35.
8. *Ibid.*, pp. 181-93.
9. *Ibid.*, p. 182.
10. *Ibid.*, pp. 182-83.
11. *Ibid.*, p. 185.
12. *Ibid.*, pp. 186-87.
13. *Ibid.*, p. 190.
14. *Ibid.*, p. 191.
15. *Ibid.*, p. 192.
16. *Men of the Mountains*, pp. 205-25.
17. *Ibid.*, p. 222.
18. *The Clearing in the Sky*, (New York, 1950), pp. 118-33.
19. *Plowshare in Heaven*, pp. 73-83.
20. *Head O' W-Hollow* (New York, 1936), pp. 129-49.
21. *Men of the Mountains*, pp. 336-349.
22. *Tales from the Plum Grove Hills*, pp. 73-80.
23. *Head O' W-Hollow*, pp. 210-231.
24. *Ibid.*, pp. 67-92.
25. *Ibid.*, pp. 93-104.
26. *Tales from the Plum Grove Hills*, pp. 194-209.
27. *Head O' W-Hollow*, pp. 6-22.
28. *Ibid.*, pp. 150-192.

29. *Tales from the Plum Grove Hills,* pp. 13-21.
30. *Ibid.,* pp. 117-129.
31. *Ibid.,* pp. 181-193.
32. *Ibid.,* pp. 224-232.
33. *Ibid.,* p. 52.
34. *Clearing in the Sky,* pp. 32-41.
35. First published in *Esquire,* VIII (August, 1937), 36-37, 182-84, 187-88 Published in book form in Edward J. O'Brien (ed.), *The Best Short Stories 1938,* (New York and Boston, 1938), pp. 288-305.
36. "Huey, the Engineer," O'Brien, *op. cit.,* p. 305.

Chapter Four

1. *Trees of Heaven* (New York, 1940), p. 340.
2. His description of caring for newly born lambs was excerpted from the novel, reprinted, and circulated to farmers during World War II by the U.S. Department of Agriculture because of its value for sheep raisers.
3. News note in a Louisville, Kentucky, newspaper. Cf. Microfilm of Stuart Scrapbooks, *Scrapbooks* 82-92.
4. Letter from Stuart to the author, August 4, 1965.
5. Cf., for instance, Faulkner's boy narrator in *The Reivers.*
6. The above facts and the quotation are from a letter by Stuart to the author, July 23, 1965.
7. *Foretaste of Glory* (New York, 1946), p. 13.

Chapter Five

1. Stuart was carrying this manuscript to mail it to his publishers when a sharp wind blew it from his hands. It would have blown under a train and been chopped up had not Senator A. B. Chandler who was nearby stamped on it with his foot. Stuart remarks that he is the only writer in the country who has a manuscript bearing the shoeprint of a governor, U.S. senator, and baseball commissioner.
2. *Mongrel Mettle* (New York, 1944), p. 71.
3. *Hie to the Hunters* (New York, 1950), pp. 68-69.
4. Stuart says his regular publisher turned this novel down because the boy ran away from home, but McGraw-Hill picked it up and published it.
5. Cf. Stuart's "Under My Sky" in the *Louisville Courier Journal,* November 30, 1957.
6. *The Good Spirit of Laurel Ridge* (New York, 1963), p. 121.

Chapter Six

1. Paraphrase from a letter by Stuart (May 18, 1963, Greenup, Ky.) to Woodridge Spears in Georgetown, Ky.

Selected Bibliography

PRIMARY SOURCES

Man with a bull-tongue Plow. New York: E. P. Dutton & Co., 1934.
Head O' W-Hollow. New York: E. P. Dutton & Co., 1936.
Beyond Dark Hills. New York: E. P. Dutton & Co., 1938.
Trees of Heaven. New York: E. P. Dutton & Co., 1940.
Men of the Mountains. New York: E. P. Dutton & Co., 1941.
Taps For Private Tussie. New York: E. P. Dutton & Co., 1943.
Mongrel Mettle. New York: Books Inc., E. P. Dutton & Co., 1944.
Album of Destiny. New York: E. P. Dutton & Co., 1944.
Foretaste of Glory. New York: E. P. Dutton & Co., 1946.
Tales from the Plum Grove Hills. New York: E. P. Dutton & Co., 1946.
The Thread That Runs So True. New York: Charles Scribner's Sons, 1949.
Hie to the Hunters. New York: Whittlesey House, 1950.
Clearing in the Sky. New York: McGraw-Hill Book Co., 1950.
Kentucky Is My Land. New York: E. P. Dutton & Co., 1952.
The Good Spirit of Laurel Ridge. New York: McGraw-Hill Book Co., 1953.
The Beatinest Boy. New York: Whittlesey House, 1953.
A Penny's Worth of Character. New York: Whittlesey House, 1954.
Red Mule. New York: Whittlesey House, 1955.
The Year of My Rebirth. New York: McGraw-Hill Book Co., 1956.
Plowshare in Heaven. New York: McGraw-Hill Book Co., 1958.
God's Oddling. New York: McGraw-Hill Book Co., 1960.
Huey the Engineer. St. Helena, California: James E. Beard, 1960.
The Rightful Owner. New York: Whittlesey House, 1960.
Andy Finds a Way. New York: Whittlesey House, 1961.
Hold April. New York: McGraw-Hill Book Co., 1962.
A Jesse Stuart Reader. New York: McGraw-Hill Book Co., 1963.
Save Every Lamb. New York: McGraw-Hill Book Co., 1964.
Daughter of the Legend. New York: McGraw-Hill Book Co., 1965.
My Land Has a Voice. New York: McGraw-Hill Book Co., 1966.
Mr. Gallion's School. New York: McGraw-Hill Book Co., 1967.

SECONDARY SOURCES

BLAIR, EVERETTA LOVE. "Jesse Stuart and His Work: A Critical Study." Unpublished thesis, University of South Carolina, 1954.

Selected Bibliography

LEAVELL, FRANK HARTWELL. "The Literary Career of Jesse Stuart." Unpublished Ph.D. dissertation, Vanderbilt University, 1966.

MITCHELL, BEULAH. "A Study of the Life and Works of Jesse Stuart." Unpublished thesis, East Texas State Teacher's College, 1952.

RAMEY, LEE OLY. "An Inquiry into the Life of Jesse Stuart as Related to His Literary Development and a Critical Study of His Works." Unpublished M.A. thesis, Ohio University, 1941.

ROSE, MARY GLENN. "Jesse Stuart: Pioneer Writer of the Kentucky Hills." Unpublished thesis, George Peabody College for Teachers, 1938.

WASHINGTON, MARY. "The Folklore of the Cumberlands as Reflected in the Writings of Jesse Stuart." Unpublished Ph.D. dissertation, University of Pennsylvania, 1960.

WOODBRIDGE, HENSLEY C. *Jesse Stuart: A Bibliography.* Harrogate, Tenn.: Lincoln Memorial University Press, 1960.

———, *Jesse Stuart: A Bibliography for May, 1960–May, 1965.*

73310

Index

73310

818.52
F756

DATE DUE

GAYLORD			PRINTED IN U.S.A.